The Lead Guitarist & The Sisterhood of the Wolf

Also By Gregory Drambour:

The Woodstock Bridge

The Shaman & His Daughter

The Lead Guitarist
& The Sisterhood
of the Wolf

Gregory Drambour

SB

SACRED BEAR PRESS

Published by Sacred Bear Press, a division of Sedona Sacred Journeys, LLC

ISBN: 9781792124419

FIRST EDITION

Cover Wolf Photograph "Amber" used with permission of Shari Jardina
Guitar Player Photograph used with permission of iStock
Design: Anugito, Artline Graphics
Cover Idea by Kelsey Erin Sky

For Robert Johnson & Jimi Hendrix,
you played and I heard, brothers.

For the beautiful wolf on the cover
for opening the door to the story.
I am deeply honored by your friendship.

AUTHOR'S NOTE

What follows are a few suggestions from your humble author to make the book really come alive while you read. The first - and most important - is that you download the song "Are You Experienced" from Jimi Hendrix's first album, *Are You Experienced*, and listen before you turn this page and begin Chapter One. Then go ahead and turn the page as the song is playing. Trust me on this! It will give the story another powerful dimension and really make you feel it. Then, brothers and sisters, I encourage you to let the music of the sixties and early seventies be in the background as your close companion while you read.

As part of your playlist, please include the music of Robert Johnson, the king of the Delta blues.

A Ho.
Gregory Drambour
Magic Kingdom (Sedona), AZ
December 2018

CHAPTER ONE
James Ryder

We all have something special inside us; the challenge is believing in it and letting our uniqueness come out. My dad was the first person to see my talent. And since I was a kid, folks that came in and out of my life also recognized it. The gift is separated into two parts, which makes it complicated. One side, I express with joyful abandon. The other half is like a prisoner inside me waiting to be set free. I hold the cell-door shut tight like my life depends on it, and that keeps me under a dark cloud of self-judgment.

My name is James Ryder. I'm twenty-eight years old, and it's 1986. The uniqueness inside me I do let soar free is the way I play electric guitar. There's no way of stopping it – it's a wild, uncontrollable force. The other gift that has been waiting to be released for twenty years is my own original music. I call them musical whispers. They started flowing out when I got my first guitar at eight years old.

For five years, I've lived in New York City, making my living playing guitar on the street. It's the only place

I will let myself play – where I feel safe playing. No one can touch these musical whispers inside me there. And they do feel like whispers that are coming from somewhere deep within. I've only been able to describe it as a feeling like I've *forgotten something*. My dad was the one person I was able to share that strange thought with.

He's gone six years now, and my mom passed when I was one year old – both from cancer. My dad was my best friend and my biggest fan. He was a tough-guy, worked as a supervisor on the line at General Motors. Hard-core work ethic. Respected. When he passed, some part of me left too. Of course, I want to make him proud of me. His wish for me was to show people the music that's inside of me. But I'm not able to share it, and I can't figure out why. So, I wait for the cell-door to open.

I live in a one-room apartment in an old brownstone building on the Upper West Side. If you walked into my apartment, you would think it was a teenager's room from the late sixties or early seventies, with worn posters of the bands and concerts from that era covering most of the four walls in a collage – Led Zeppelin, Hendrix, Steppenwolf, Cream, The Who, The Allman Brothers, Rare Earth, The Doors. It's like an explosion of psychedelic colors that shield me from the outside world. In one corner of the room stands a very old acoustic guitar that's my soul. On the floor sits weathered amplifiers and microphones that feel like friends to me. An old pull-out phonograph rests on top of four wooden crates crammed with my collection of vintage records. Littered about the room are Zeppelin and Hendrix music books – my bibles. On the metal-framed bed is my Fender Strato-caster electric guitar – my brother. He's watched over by a framed photograph of me and my dad with his arm supportively around my shoulders; we're standing next to his baby – a pristine 1967 black Corvette. This is my sanctuary. It's all I need, at least that's what I've con-vinced myself.

Since I can remember, at least once a week, I wake up in the middle of the night from a recurring nightmare. It starts the same way, with images charging at me from the powerful "Are You Experienced" video by Jimi Hen-drix – which is an intense series of flash-like scenes of Hendrix in concert intertwined with psychedelic images of Jimi. His electric guitar and voice are pushing at me from all sides, like they're trying to pierce some deep part of me – as if the sound is trying to open a door inside me. Over and over again, Hendrix is singing the song, "Are You Experienced?" Then, suddenly, I'm walking through a forest shrouded in a heavy mist. I look ahead and see a small clearing, and barely visible in the fog stands a dilapidated white shack. Sitting out front are seven empty straight-back wooden chairs forming a quarter-circle. The chairs seem to be waiting. Then I'm thrust back into the "Are You Experienced" video – physically running through the clips of Hendrix in concert. He's wailing on his Stratocaster with his usual focused wildness – the images of him pass by me in a rush. Then a picture of an old Native American woman flashes in front of me; she's standing by the side of a two-lane paved road surrounded by open plains. She smiles at me as if she knows me. I hear Native drumming in the distance. And then, quickly, I'm back in the woods, this time running fast. I sense someone running next to me but can't really see them. I feel afraid as if I am being chased. A gunshot cracks in the air – something whizzes by my ear. The shock of it forces me awake. For a moment, I'm not sure where I am – I'm scared. I try to look around my room to orient myself with what's familiar – the picture of me and my dad, my guitars…slowly, the fear fades. Not the best way to wake up. But sometimes after the nightmare, I'm inspired to pick up my acoustic guitar and write a new song, but again the thought of sharing it terrifies me.

I wrote the dream down and studied it in hopes that I could understand its meaning – nothing came to me. But I know it *means something*, brothers and sisters, I know it's important. Why? Because, like many other guitarists, my teacher and inspiration are part of the dream – Jimi Hendrix. What is the mysterious connection between him and the shack in the woods?

I have spent my life studying Jimi. There is not a book written about him that I have not read or one of his songs I haven't learned. But the answer still alludes me.

CHAPTER TWO
James Ryder

It's Wednesday in the spring, about 7:00 a.m. Little did I know, a hard, westerly wind was coming and in a few days my whole life would change. I'm getting ready to head down to Wall Street where I will set up to play for the day. Every morning, it's the same ritual: with great care and a sense of formality, I place my Stratocaster in its black, soft-leather guitar case, loop it carefully over my shoulder, always liking the weight of my guitar on my back, feeling a little like a character in a movie venturing out on an adventure. I pick up my small portable amplifier, take a deep breath, and open the apartment door and walk down the hallway, which hasn't seen a coat of paint in a while.

One apartment door down, I see Robert, a ten-year-old boy that I've gotten close to over the last few years. No matter how bad my dreams are or how deeply frustrated I get, he makes me smile. He's thin, with longish, straight brown hair, and has a New York City toughness and quick wit but also a deep intuitiveness that can be startling.

"Hey, Robert," I call out to him.

"James, can I come today? I practiced all night." The words tumble over each other, rushing to get it out. I have been giving him guitar lessons since he and his mother moved in. He's good. Better than me at that age.

"All night?" I smile and exclaim in disbelief. This is our usual morning banter.

"Well, until my mom locked my guitar in the closet."

"What's today?" I ask to remind him.

"Wednesday," he blurts out quickly, trying to suppress a giggle.

"And what usually happens on Wednesday?"

"You got me." He shrugs his little shoulders with conviction. I see the sparkle in his brown eyes.

"It's the same thing that happens on Mondays!"

"Can you give me a hint?" He tries to hold back a laugh. The game is to see who can break first.

"Well, this only happens during the week, not on weekends," I explain, as if talking to someone who doesn't understand the process.

"It only happens during the week?" He questions me with a totally straight face, his forehead furrowing as if he's trying to understand. He's good at this and might even have potential as an actor.

"Yeah, you go to this big building, and they lock all the little kids in there till three o'clock in the afternoon," I respond like it's no big deal.

He conjures up a look of terror and says, "What do

they do in there? It sounds pretty horrible. You wouldn't let them get me, right?"

I respond, giving him more information, "Well, they have these groups."

"Groups?" he answers, confused.

"Yeah, they get a bunch of people together in one room and they tell them how to do different things." I try and make it sound enticing.

"What kind of things do they tell you? I mean, I don't want to get trapped with a bunch of weirdos." A corner of his lip curls up to show his distaste for "weirdos."

"Well you see, that's the problem with this place. You can't find out unless you go."

"What kind of rip-off is that?" he asks, with a perfect imitation of being affronted. I feel a laugh surging up in me, but I press my lips together to hold it in.

"I know it's a bummer, but what can you do? I hear that it's not too bad. In fact, you feel pretty good after it's over. Why don't you give it a shot? You know, just hang out, see what happens."

"Did you hang out at this place when you were a kid?" He questions me seriously, like he's taking a survey. Total poker-face.

"No, I was born a grown-up, so I was excused from going!" I laugh, finally breaking our ritual morning "bs" session.

His apartment door opens, and his mother steps out in the hallway with us. She's in her early forties, petite, with kind, supportive eyes. You can tell she's seen some rough times. I'm not sure of what the history is, but whatever happened makes me admire this woman – survivor is written all over her.

"Morning, James," she says sweetly. She is always nice to me, which means more than I can tell her.

"Morning, Mrs. Conner," I answer, smiling.

"Is Robert holding you up again?" she asks, concerned.

"No, no, not at all, ma'am." One thing about my dad, he might have been a little rough, but he was a stickler for politeness and formality – it was always, "Yes, sir" and "No, ma'am."

"James, you're going to call me Joan if it's the last thing I do!

"Sorry," I say, grinning, appreciating her need to make me feel comfortable.

"Don't see you around much." I can see the worry in her eyes.

"I guess I stay in a lot," I respond, in a way I hope doesn't offend her.

She glances down at Robert and says firmly, "Time to get ready for school."

"Okay," Robert says, resigned to his fate, then asks me, "See you tonight, right?"

"You got it," I assure him. I raise my fist in front of my chest in our traditional salute, and he returns it with the utmost seriousness – the brotherhood of the guitar.

As Robert walks into the apartment, his mother shouts after him, "And leave your guitar where I left it!" She turns to me and says, smiling, "He got a little loud last night. The windows were rattling!" We laugh. "Thanks for all your help with him...spending time with him." I see some pain flash in her eyes, but I'm not sure what it's about.

"No problem." I feel grateful to help this woman, even though it's Robert who really helps me. His innocence takes me out of the darkness for a little while.

Joan asks me, "Where to today?"

"Wall Street," I say, feeling it might be good there today. Each place I play has good and bad days.

"Stay safe," she says, and then adds, "Will you come for dinner soon?"

"Absolutely. See you later." I head down the stairs to the subway feeling a little better about the world.

CHAPTER THREE
James Ryder

The subway car is crowded. I squeeze myself in an opening between folks, trying not to poke anyone with my guitar or amp. Not sure what it is about being a street musician, but people always seem to smile at me. There is a friendliness in their energy when they see me going to or coming from where I set up for the day. They want to be helpful.

To pass the time, I glance up and study the ads and see one for an upcoming Eric Clapton concert at Madison Square Garden. I hang out for a moment in my imagination, seeing Clapton on stage, 25,000 concertgoers digging on his music. That's when I feel the familiar, severe disappointment in myself rush up deep within and, as usual, I grip it tightly, holding onto it – maybe hoping if I feel the self-judgment long enough and intensely enough, I will find an answer.

I get off the subway and walk over to the crossroads of Wall/Nassau/Broad streets. This corner is surrounded by tightly grouped towering buildings; it's the middle of the New York Financial District – great acoustics. A silence comes into my Spirit as I begin to set up. I slowly unzip my guitar case, take out my guitar as if I were handling a sacred object, drape the guitar strap ceremoniously over my body, and then lay the case open on the sidewalk where hopefully passersby will deposit money. I plug into the amplifier, turn it on, feeling my guitar connect into the psychical space around me. I can always feel my body breathing in these moments – my consciousness moves into a stillness within myself. I scan around, absorbing the people around me, rushing to their offices. And then I begin to play, always and forever starting with a Led Zeppelin song, paying homage to my elders. On this day, it's "Dazed and Confused" – not sure why, it's just instinct. With each chord, I sense the area become congested as the stampede to work ramps up. People pour out of the subway entrances and buses, jump out of taxies – hurrying, oblivious of me. It's okay, they never see me this early, I'm used to it. The gathering storm of notes of "Dazed and Confused" seems to move in rhythm with the mounting tension in the street. I'm losing myself like I have since I was a kid. The guitar and I are one. I lean my head back, close my eyes, feel the notes firing off my fingers, and then I'm finally home inside my Spirit.

CHAPTER FOUR

Char Montgomery

My name is Char Montgomery – a name I'm hon-ored to carry. I grew up on a working ranch in Montana where pride in your work means something. Some people will tell you I'm one tough cowgirl – maybe that's how I got to where I am in the music busi-ness at such a young age. I'm twenty-nine years old, tall and thin but strong in the bone with a dark-brown, thick pony-tail hanging down my back. I'm a full-fledged record producer with R&R Records in New York City – a top-flight company. They hired me because they say I have the "ear." When I came on board, they asked me what I wanted. It's simple: to bring back the music that was lost. Where are the Led Zeppelins today? Where is the original voice? I'm here to tell you on this beautiful year of the Lord, 1986, I will find those musicians. I'm tasked by the higher-ups in the record company to put together a band that reflects the vision I have in my mind. I won't let up until they're together and playing a major venue. I didn't give up when I was twelve years old out in the Montana wilderness by myself and surrounded by a pack of wolves. My adopted grandfather, a Crow elder, taught me how to *turn into a wolf* – and when I did, the other wolves just went about their business because I looked just like one of them. Their Spirit lives in me, and it will lead me to the music that speaks to the mysteries inside all of us.

It's Wednesday in May and I'm standing in Grand Central Train Station, one of my favorite places in the city – history oozes out of the architecture. I'm watching a saxophone player doing his thing; he is absolutely tapping into his soul as the melodic sax sounds waft through the station. He's in his early forties, dressed nicely with a cool vibe. I just let the sounds of the horn wash over me, letting it calm me, because today I'm on my mission. He finishes, and several people stop and drop money in his case. I feel happy others *get* this cat.

I walk up and drop a ten-dollar bill in his case. He looks up, surprised, and says, "Wow, thanks!"

"Son, you have a beautiful sound." I hope he hears I mean it. Even though I have been in New York a while, I can't seem to lose the Western way of speaking.

"Thank you," he responds, ducking his head with a wonderful humility that is so refreshing to experience as opposed to some of the egos I have to deal with.

"The acoustics in here are amazing," I comment, glancing up at the high-dome ceilings.

"I know!" he says, sharing my feeling.

"That's a fine-looking horn." I study his saxophone,

and the deep love he has for it is obvious.

"Thanks for noticing. We've seen some times together." The history of that journey is evident in his voice.

"I can see that." I pause a moment. "Hey, maybe you can help me. I'm looking for this guitarist." I try to keep my voice calm, even though every cell in my body is vibrating.

"He plays the street?" he asks.

"Yeah, exactly."

"I know most of them," he says. A spark of hope fires off in me.

"I think his name is James Ryder." At the mention of his name, I see a serious emotion pass over the sax player's face.

"Yeah, I know who you mean. He's good. He's been playing the street for a couple years."

"Do you know where I can find him?" I'm jumping out of my skin at this point but pull it back quickly. I intuitively sense my Wolf-Sister totem materialize next to me – she has thick black fur with the most amazing amber eyes. She sharpens her focus, hearing we might get a lead on this guitarist. And when wolves get focused, there is no stopping them! She and I have traveled together for almost twenty years. I go – she goes. She is my partner, best friend, and my inspiration. If you are not familiar with animal totems, they live in the *Dreamweave*, which is a Native American word for alternative universe.

The sax player says, "No, he moves around a lot, keeps to himself. Won't play with anyone. I asked him once."

"Really?"

"Sometimes we try to team up for protection." He hesitates as I watch him thinking. "Hey, you know, once I did see him with this black kid. He plays on one of those upside-down pails – like the drums. It was some pretty heavy stuff."

"What do you mean?" My whole being is listening to his response. I can see him trying to find the words, and I witness him go back into that emotional place the same way he did when I first mentioned James's name.

He peers directly in my eyes, holding them in his gaze, and just repeats with emphasis, "Heavy."

I nod, understanding his silent message. "Do you remember where you saw them?"

"Maybe it was Time Square. If not, try the subway platforms around there."

"Okay. Thanks so much. I really appreciate it."

"Sure, no problem," he says.

"Hope I see you again," I say as I walk away, the excitement buzzing in me. I can hear the sax player flowing into some high-speed bebop. My Wolf-Sister walks in step with me as we move towards our dream.

CHAPTER FIVE

Char Montgomery

B ack in the office, I head past the main reception desk. It's a classic record company with all their gold and platinum albums on the walls – mostly boy bands and solo artists, nobody with any teeth. Contemporary furniture all around the place, not a lot of warmth.

Annie, our receptionist, greets me. It's always good to see her smiling face. The atmosphere can get a little hostile here.

"Hey Char!"

"What's up, beautiful?" She is gorgeous!

I hurry past the big desk and head to my office, passing another friend, Scott, who's in his late twenties like me. He's a genius behind the sound board.

"Char Montgomery! The best producer in New York! Wow, what's happening?" he announces, as if he hasn't just seen me this morning at a recording session. Some of the staff's upbeat attitude is one of the reasons I keep hanging in here.

"Get back to work, slacker!" I respond, laughing.

I see the assistant to my boss, the president of the

company, walking towards me. Oh, shit, I think. His
name is Eric, and he's in his mid-thirties with a business
school degree, and he looks the part – I've never seen
him out of a suit. He doesn't like me, and I don't like
him.

I greet him flatly. "Eric."

"Mr. Chandler wants a progress report on the pack-
aging of your band as soon as possible." There is a snide
self-importance to every word that comes out of this
guy's mouth. I'd like to see how he handles being in a
cabin in the "high-up" back home with a 40-mph bliz-
zard blowing, and he has to go outside with the temper-
ature at minus 15 degrees and chop some wood so he
doesn't freeze to death.

I hold myself back, responding again totally without
emotion. You could iron a shirt on my words. "Yes, I
know, I'll have it on his desk in an hour." I can sense my
Wolf-Sister next to me starting to growl; she doesn't do
well with humans who are getting aggressive with me.
In my mind, I tell her, *Easy, girl, easy.*

Then he decides to push it and says, "You found a
lead guitar yet?" The condescension dripping from his
question.

I shake my head, still holding back. This cat still does-
n't get I won't be talked to like this.

He continues, "Still looking for that guy in the
street?" Big tone-emphasis on "street."

I take one step closer, just staring at him. My Wolf-

Sister is starting to bare her teeth. Even though people can't see her, they can sometimes feel her emotion. If you've never seen a wolf do this, I'm here to tell you it's a frightening sight.

He adds sarcastically, "Why not try the clubs? You usually find guitarists there."

I stare hard, unblinking at him. He moves back, and I detect a subtle little nervousness in his eyes. Then I say, smiling, "You were the bully on the playground, weren't you?" I look him up and down, assessing his worth. "You have no idea how excited that makes me. See you around the campfire, hoss."

He seems stunned, scared, but not really understanding why.

I break off, turn the corner, and stride down to my office. I sense him frozen to his spot. My Wolf-Sister pulls backs, and I can see the kickass expression of satisfaction on her face. As if she's about to say, "We are the Sisterhood of the Wolf, are you kidding me!"

Up ahead is my office watched over by my guardian angel, Marie, a voluptuous red-headed stunner with full pouty lips, who does not date musicians!

She hands me my messages and asks with a hopeful voice, "Any luck, Char?"

"No, but I've got a couple of leads. I'll find him. I'm close, I can feel it." What Eric the jerk doesn't understand about me is that his kind of negative nonsense just gets me more determined.

"Did you try the subways yet?" Marie asks. She's emotionally invested in this as much as I am. That's why she is who she is – a friend who's got my back.

"Tomorrow, Red, tomorrow!" I open the door to my office and go in.

I hear her yell at me, "Stop calling me Red!" This is a joke with us. She loves it.

I close the door and take a deep breath, feeling safe to relax. My office is a special place to me. I made it my own. I sit down behind my big, old ornate desk that dates back a hundred years. It's from home and was taken out of a saloon; the boss didn't like it, but I feel I have a little leverage since the company tracked me down to work for them based on my taste in music, not furniture! The senior executives do seem to dig my daily attire of jeans, cowboy boots, a flannel shirt, and my Montana State Champ Bronco Rodeo belt-buckle, which I got when I was a teenager. On the walls are a dozen framed posters of the great groups from the sixties and early seventies that inspired me. Some of them are even signed by the members of the band. Each of them keeps me in the pocket, reminding me to stay focused on what I'm creating and to not make compromises. There is a powerful deep musical *sound* that's in my Spirit – I hear it so clearly. Musicians had a feeling of authenticity back in the early days of heavy rock until the corporate machine took over. One thing I am sure of: I will *know* that sound when I hear it.

In the teak bookshelves against the wall, you'll find every single book written by my favorite writer, Louis L'Amour. I have read every one more times than I can count – just in one page of reading, I'm transported back home to the West. Also, on the walls are four framed photographs of wolves; my favorite is one that resembles my Wolf-Sister, a mysterious black wolf with amber eyes peeking between two trees. These photos help keep the Spirit of the wolf alive in me.

I flip through my messages, nothing of any interest. I feel disappointed that there are no leads on James, the guitarist. I turn to the place I'm sure will inspire me to keep pushing: my stereo system. I glance down and see *Physical Graffiti* by Led Zeppelin on the platter of the Garrard turntable. I cue up the tone arm and watch it hit the record and hear "In the Light" flow out of my KHL speakers. I love this song, but as I stare at the record spinning around, a concern flashes up inside me: *Am I going to make the band happen?* Leaning against the wall on the other side of the room behind me is *my talisman*; my adopted Crow. Grandfather would call it my "Medicine," the source my power comes from. I turn slowly, always shocked to see it there – a rectangular, black guitar case, the worn leather of the cover peeling here and there; it stands upright against the wall under my black wolf photograph – waiting. I call across to what's *inside* the case, "Soon, brother, soon."

CHAPTER SIX
James Ryder

It's lunch time now on Wall Street, and folks are form-ing little groups around me listening. It always makes me happy but, at the same time, a little nervous – not sure why I feel this way still after all these years. I move into a Steppenwolf song, "Magic Carpet Ride," and I can sense the street crowd move in rhythm to my guitar's riffs in the air.

When people drop money in the guitar case, I try my best to acknowledge them with a nod or smile or mouthing thanks – always feeling a little shy.

I look around, checking out different folks, and notice a policeman moving his fingers covertly on his nightstick like he's playing a guitar. I think, *How cool!* Three busi-ness-suited men in their late thirties pass by, one of them plays "air drums." I give him a big grin, appreciating his connection. Two young blue-coated male pages from the Stock Exchange drop money in the case and give me a fist-salute, which I return. Two teenage girls bop by and start giggling – not sure about what, but they drop money in the case quickly and scoot off with further giggles.

All the days playing on the street are not as connecting and positive as today. Sometimes, you can get some weird vibes and negative people.

I decide to take a break for lunch and buy a hotdog and coke from one of the vendors and sit on some steps, just watching the world go by. I notice a man in his early fifties, about six foot, strong-looking, kind of reminiscent of my dad, with lots of energy as he walks and talks animatedly with his seventeen-year-old son. The man seems completely okay with who he is; he's wearing an Elvis T-shirt, and he and his son are laughing – you can see the deep rapport between them. My dad loved Elvis – never stopped going on about him. When I was in my teens, I'd be practicing on weekends in the garage that I had turned into my own studio, and he would swing open the big garage door so he could watch me as he detailed his '67 black Corvette. As my guitar sound poured through the neighborhood, he would yell with glee over my guitar, "Let the neighbors complain!" Sometimes he couldn't hold himself back and mimic along, playing "air guitar." We would trade imaginary licks back and forth. Then I would segue into an Elvis tune, like "Jailhouse Rock." This would cue my Dad to dance the twist, embarrassing me which he took great pleasure in. We would belt out the song, trying our best to reach the high notes.

When we were done, he'd shout to the neighborhood, "Elvis Presley!"

Then together we'd proclaim so there was no doubt, "The king of rock and roll!"

"Study Elvis, kiddo. He had the stuff – one of the guys that started it."

"I know, Dad, I know. You told me...

"...A million times," we'd finish together. His son was not going to not get Elvis!

I would ask him if he had heard the new melody I was working on.

Always a similar answer, "Yeah, sounded great, real rock-blues vibe!" His excitement encouraged me to let my own music out. I put together a half-dozen songs I felt proud of, but he was the *only one* I let hear them.

I used to tell him about the experience of writing music: "It's the same strange feeling, Dad, like I have heard the sound before."

"Don't worry about it, just let it come," he would encourage me.

Then one day when I was nineteen, he raced into the house, super-psyched, and said, "Hey, I stopped by that recording studio today. I saw a sign for a band that's looking for someone to play lead guitar."

I just shook my head. The thought of sharing my music with anyone terrified me.

He asked, "What's the problem?"

I told him "I'm just not ready yet," and hoped he'd

drop the whole idea.

But he persisted, saying, "You're terrific! Give it a shot."

When I didn't respond, he kept pressing me, asking, "What are you worried about?"

"I don't know."

"I think you do."

"Maybe I'm no good!" I yelled.

He looked at me confused, baffled why I would think that. I wondered too – I knew I had some talent, but something was stopping me, a dark feeling that haunted me when I played. I wasn't ready to reveal so much of myself. I tried to figure out some way to get him detoured: "Dad, these people aren't going to understand my music, I'm not even sure I do."

He would say, "Don't worry about it, some day you will, I promise you. Just be you and let it out."

Then I yelled, "Don't you think it's all I think about and dream about? Playing in front of thousands of people, taking them with me, flying. I want that so much. Why do I feel so afraid?"

"Son, you have something special. You can do it. I know you can." He said this with such unbending confidence that some part of me wanted to believe him. It was like he knew something about me that even I didn't know. It felt like more than just parental encouragement. That's how it was between us. He was my cheerleader.

My memories fade, and I'm back on the street, watching the end of the day come and people hurry home to their families. Even though fewer folks drop money in the case, I continue to play. Soon, it's just me and the pigeons and a handful of pedestrians. At these times, my playing gets even more intense. I become more deeply lost in the music and find myself staring off into the nothingness, feeling a wanting, a sadness – *feeling something* "out there." For a lot of years, I've tried to understand what these feelings meant, but the answers never came.

CHAPTER SEVEN
James Ryder

Later that night, I'm sitting on my apartment floor, leaning against the bed, singing some lyrics that flowed up in me earlier, playing a rhythm on my special acoustic guitar that keeps *whispering* to me. Since seeing that father in the street earlier, I began to feel my dad's energy, and it's even stronger tonight – sadness has got a hold of me but not as bad as it can get; it used to paralyze me. I hear a knock on the door.

"It's Robert," he says on the other side. It's guitar-lesson time.

"Door's open," I yell out to him.

He walks in carrying a small electric guitar.

"Hey, what's happening?" As I greet him, I try to pull back any sadness he might vibe from me.

"Thanks for talking to my mom," he says sheepishly, sitting in his usual chair.

"Sure. Just keep the volume below concert level, okay?"

"I promise," he assures me. I can tell he's sincere and not just appeasing me.

He studies me a moment, squinting his eyes, and then says solemnly, "You're missing your dad, huh?" So much for my covering! This kid is way too perceptive. It's almost otherworldly.

"Yeah," I say, trying to shake the sadness off. "Your dad's coming to see you soon, right?" I ask, trying to deflect the conversation away from me and my dad.

"This weekend." I hear a slight worry in his voice as he looks down at his electric guitar lying across his lap.

"Great!" I say positively. There have been some issues with his dad not showing, so I don't want him to get too much in his head about it.

"We're going to spend the whole day together," he responds, but his face tells me he's not convinced.

"You guys will have a lot of fun," I assure him.

"I wish you could come," he says quietly, eyes cast at the floor. I can feel his fear of being disappointed. He holds his guitar tightly against his chest as if to protect himself. My heart aches for this kid.

"Well, it's best if it's just you and your dad. You know, father and son stuff."

"Yeah, I guess," he says, his voice barely audible. The more we talk about this, the more I see the energy draining out of him, so I switch the subject quickly.

"Show me what you been practicing," I tell him, brightening my voice.

Robert's spirit lifts like a shot; anxious to show me, he plugs his guitar into an amp and stands in his favorite spot by the old phonograph. He plays a series of chords, finishing with a rock-guitarist flair and looks up at me for the verdict.

"Outstanding!" I proclaim.

His eyes light up, and the lingering sadness in me is gone in an instant. I plug my Fender Stratocaster into another amplifier.

"Okay, here's a new one for you." I play a series of chords, then Robert tries to imitate. He flubs it and, with a mock pout, appeals to me show him again.

"Okay, watch closely." I show him, going slow with my finger movements, "You see that change?"

"How much money did you make today?" he asks. I had a suspicion this flubbing was just a ruse; he likes hearing about my day.

"Not enough! Let's get back on it."

"James, tell me about the day you saw the guitar." He points to my acoustic guitar lying on the bed. "When you were a kid like me." His love for this story shines in his eyes, and I think he likes hearing about my dad and me.

"You've heard it a hundred times!"

"Please," he whines.

Jesus, I think, smiling, *I'm too easy on this kid's practice-discipline.*

"All right! I was eight years old, and I was walking down the street with my dad, and he went into a store and told me to wait outside, he'd be right back. So, I waited for a little while and I got bored and walked a ways down the street. Suddenly, something inside of me, it was like a little voice, told me to go around the corner."

"Weren't you afraid you'd get in trouble?" he asks, a fearful tone in his voice, like he's on the street with me that day.

"Sure. That's why I didn't do anything right away. I just stood there, but the voice inside got louder and louder, and no matter how hard I tried to ignore it, it wouldn't go away. Finally, I couldn't stand it anymore, and so I walked around the corner. On the other side was a music store. I remember I peered in the window and saw this guitar, and I got this strange feeling inside that I had seen it before, but I couldn't remember when. It was very old, kind of beaten up, and it looked lonely. All the other instruments in the window disappeared, and all I saw was this guitar." I space out for a moment, lost in the memory.

Anxious for me to keep going, Robert blurts out, "This is the best part! Don't stop!"

I snap back to the story.

"I kept staring at the guitar, and the feeling that I had forgotten something got stronger and stronger. And I remember thinking that what I had forgotten was very sad. It was like the guitar was talking to me."

"Cool!" Robert says, and then adds hesitantly, as if telling me a secret he's not sure he wants to share. "My guitar talks to me too."

"I had a feeling it did, partner." I rustle his hair, showing him how much alike we are and that he's not alone.

"Then your dad showed up, right?" he asks, his tone rising in alarm.

"Yup. He came running around the corner. Man, he was angry. I remember, I turned away from the guitar and raised my eyes up at him, and he just stopped in his tracks. It was strange, his face got real serious, and he stared at me and then the guitar in the window for what seemed a long time. Then, he walked into the store and bought it. He came out, got down to my height, handed the guitar to me flat across his palms, and said in this kind-of-emotional voice, "Never forget where you came from, son."

Robert cocks his head and asks, "What did that mean?" The need to understand that I heard in his voice had the same urgency as the question I had asked myself.

"I don't know," I say, shaking my head in confusion, brought back to that day twenty years ago. I gaze more purposely into Robert's eyes to share with him what my dad said so that he himself can share in my dad's answer. "He said, one day it would make sense to me."

"Then you grew up." Robert quips, back to being a smartass New York kid. I think he is just trying to snap me out of an emotionally dark place.

"Yeah, I heard that!"

"James, how come you don't play in a band?" he asks

with a sincere curiosity. I can see by the keen focus of his eyes on me, he really wants to know.

"Does that bother you?"

"No, no. I was just thinking that people might like our stuff."

"Maybe, pal, maybe. Enough stalling. Let's get on it."

"Okay." Robert stands up and tries the new series of chords again, getting them perfect on the first try, then waits for my feedback.

"Cool! Nailed it. But once again, partner, twenty-eight demerit points for obvious deflection strategies! No practicing Hendrix for one week. Sorry, brother."

"Oh my God! Please not Hendrix, anything but that!"

CHAPTER EIGHT
James Ryder

Robert left an hour ago, getting the two signal-knocks on my wall from his mom, telling him it's time to put his guitar to bed. I sit on the bed, leaning against the wall, both guitars on either side of me; it's something I do occasionally to not feel so alone. I wonder why he asked me about being in a band. It brings back a memory that I try to forget:

My dad's persistence finally got through my resistance, and I decided to go audition for that band. Once I decided to go, I actually felt excited. The recording studio where the auditions were held was run-down and smelled really bad; there were empty beer cans littered on the floor and full ashtrays all over. Three guys in serious heavy-metal garb were waiting for me – leather pants, chains around their waist, tattoos; I got the sense right away they didn't like me. One guy, who looked to be the leader, told me where to plug in and said, "Whenever you're ready, dude." I could sense the attitude in his voice. I was not going to head home and tell my dad I didn't try, so I connected my guitar cord to the amplifier, checked the tuning on my guitar, and asked them, "What would you like to hear?"

"Do something of your own, and we'll come in," the leader said. Two of them grabbed guitars, and the other one got behind the drum kit and waited for me.

"Great," I said, showing more enthusiasm than I felt. "This is something I've been working on." I decided on a song that had come from the whispers inside me, it had that rock-blue-tone my dad referred too. I had spent dozens of hours working on it. Not the easiest arrangement to play. I started – it begins really heavy in its intensity. I figured these metal guys might like it. I got about twenty seconds in, and the leader shouted over the guitar-sound, "Heh! Hey, man!" I stopped. Then, with obvious condescension, "What was that, man?" I was stunned, I didn't know what to say. I must have turned beet-red. I just stared at him, frozen.

"We're not looking for some blues shit, bro." I heard the other musicians laugh. I felt like I was inside a fog. He said, "We're looking for speed, man." Then he rapidly fingered up and down the neck of his guitar. I just stood there, blown away.

He yells, "All right, who's next?"

When I got home, my dad was waiting in the garage/studio and asked how it went. I lost it and screamed, "NOBODY WILL EVER MESS..." I started to cry and kept saying it repeatedly as I patted my chest with the flat of my hand: "It's me, it's me..."

He grabbed me by the shoulders and said, "Look at me, kid." I raised my eyes and saw those hard-tough eyes drilling into me. "You got something special inside of you -- don't ever doubt it, not for a moment! I have never in my life heard anyone else make the sound you make, and I have seen all these great groups you have on these walls up close. But you got to share it with other people. So, they were a bunch of assholes. I'm here to tell you, son, there's a lot of them in the world. They didn't get you, who gives a shit? It doesn't mean that there aren't other musicians who won't dig it. You *don't* give up."

I told him, "I just want to be left alone. I'm happy .in the garage." It was my studio, filled with everything I loved about music – my posters, my own little sound board, the mikes, amps, and different effect pedals, and dozens of books on the great bands.

He took a moment, calming down, studying me, and said, "I tell you what. You're nineteen now. Why don't you go on a road trip across the country? It helped me when I was your age – *a lot.* Go out there and feel this country we live in, discover some things, some people. Have an adventure."

I stared at him like he was crazy and said, "What are you talking about?"

"There's more to the world than this garage you've locked yourself in since you were a kid." He hesitated, let his eyes wander around the room, landing on my special acoustic guitar for a moment, and then said with a certainty that took me aback, "I think there may be some answers out there for you."

"What answers?"

"Why don't you head down south to Mississippi. I know how much you're interested in all those old blues musicians from there, just like Hendrix was: Robert Johnson, Son House, Charley Patton, that's where they all came from."

"Mississippi?"

"And, haven't you always wanted to visit Hendrix's grave up in Seattle? You know what? Why don't you take the 'Vette!" he offers, psyched by his own idea.

"What!" That really shocked me. Even though he loved the hell out of me and trusted my driving, nobody drove his baby but him.

Three months later was when the long cancer journey began. Whatever was out there on the road had to wait.

CHAPTER NINE
James Ryder

Today, I'm down playing in the subway stations below Times Square. Probably of all the places in the city they are my favorite location – the acoustics are otherworldly with the close proximity of the tile walls. And I'm playing with Lucas, a wiry, tough, seventeen-year-old black city kid who drums on three inverted pails. Even though he's had a hard life, growing up around gangs in the projects, he's not into crime or selling drugs; I met his formidable mother once, and she wasn't a woman who would tolerate her children doing wrong. Once, a guy grabbed our money and ran, and he didn't get thirty feet before Lucas took him down. –and the thief was twice his size. The volume of sound Lucas can create with these pails is beyond comprehension. We've been playing together off and on for a few years – there is an unspoken understanding between us about our commitment to the way we both play music – with abandon. I don't know why, but when I'm playing with him, I feel freer and hold nothing back. Lucas is the same; he's very intense and completely focused on his white pails, which create a heavy, deep sound. About twenty people are standing in front of us; I usually draw the biggest crowds when Lucas is with me. We're doing some Hendrix, and I take a glance out at the audience and notice an old Native American woman watching me intently. You see very few Natives in New York. She's short, with a dark-reddish complexion, and a thick grey ponytail. She looks familiar to me. I meet her eyes and she smiles, beaming a friendliness at me that could light up a room; it's as if a warm breeze flows over me. I give her a big smile back, appreciating her silent support. Then something behind me pulls my attention and when I turn back around, she's gone. I search the crowd and the area, but there's no sign of her. Her disappearance rattles me for some reason, and I wonder if I've missed something important; I'm suddenly angry, which makes no sense to me; it feels like an old anger, one that I've carried a long time – again, I have no idea why I would discern that.

Then a desire so powerful I can't ignore it rushes up in me. I catch Lucas's attention to tell him we are changing the song, and I do something that's only happened a handful of times on the street and only when Lucas is with me – I start to play one of my own songs.

CHAPTER TEN

Char Montgomery

It's audition day here at the record company for my band. So far, I found a bass player, rhythm guitarist, and drummer. Today we're looking for the final piece – a lead guitarist. My head is not really into it, I'm just waiting to get out on the street and look for this guy, James Ryder. I heard rumors about him. He's been approached by a bunch of producers and bands, but he blows them off. The reason is unclear. But they all report the same thing: he has "something special." I study the promo-shots of guitarists while Nick, the next guy to audition, sets up. According to his resume, he's been in the music business for a while. Instead of being in the production booth, I'm hanging out with the band in one of our three recording studios. I just want to be close enough to feel the music.

I call out, "Okay, Nick, whenever you're ready. Just play whatever you feel."

He begins to play some Allman Brothers. The band knows it and comes in. Nick's guitar work is good, a little too flashy, but no real emotion in the sound. I hold up my hand after a few minutes.

"Thanks for coming in, Nick. We'll let you know."

"Thanks. See you." Nick is a journeyman, he doesn't take it personally.

When he leaves, I turn to the band for their opinion – they all shake their heads "no" in unison.

As the day wears on, I lose count of how many guitarists we've auditioned. No one even comes close to matching the sound in my soul.

Cody pipes up, "Char, I heard about this next guy, he's good." I think he senses my frustration. Cody plays rhythm guitar; at twenty-nine years old, he has a classic rocker-look -- straight black hair to his shoulders, high cheekbones, and way too good-looking! He keeps the mood light, which is important in a band dynamic. He's also super-talented and creative.

"Yeah?" I answer back, my energy a little drained out.

"That's what I heard too," George, on bass guitar, chimes in. He's thirty-two years old with dark hair and a trim beard. His wife is an angel, and they have a five-year-old boy. George is very grounded, which is important for a bass player, and plays keyboards like John Paul Jones of Zeppelin. He's a professional studio musician who is super-respected by his peers. I'm lucky to have him in the band.

A young guy, maybe twenty-five, walks in and he definitely has the look. I find his name on my list: Rich. I notice his band had a record contract with another label, but it all fell apart – tension in the band. It happens all the time.

"Hey, Rich, how's it going?"

"Real well. Thanks for having me in." Nice guy, no bullshit. Takes out a beautiful Gibson Custom Les Paul guitar – very expensive.

"You can plug in over there. Whenever you ready. Play whatever you're feeling. These guys are good, they'll follow you.

"Okay." He looks over at the band. "How about some Lynyrd Skynyrd?"

George nods, smiling – no problem. Cody, who likes to get excited about stuff, says, "Awesome! Bring on the Southern rock!" My drummer, Mark, who I'm still *iffy* about, points a drumstick at him, confirming he's got it. Mark doesn't seem a team player, which is unusual for a drummer; he's incredibly gifted – but moody. I'm trying to be patient with him. Some cats don't like the unknown, which is where we're at as we build the band.

Rich opens up, and it's obvious this guy has some real talent. The band grooves right away with him. I can see they're digging him. I let them play out the full song. They finish. Each of the band gives him an enthusiastic thumbs up.

Rich appreciates the feedback, "Thanks, guys."

I tell him, "That was awesome, Rich. We'll let you know."

"Okay. Hope to hear from you." He packs his guitar,

waves to the band, and heads out.

Cody says, "He was great."

"Yeah, that worked," adds George in that level-headed manner of his.

"Char, that guy had some chops," says Mark.

I start to pack up my stuff. "He was good, no doubt. But I got something in my head, and that's not quite it. It'll happen, guys, keep hanging in there." As I leave, I say, "I'll see you in a couple days. Red will contact you."

Cody calls after me, "Char, can I ask her out?" It's the third time he's asked me. I like his persistence!

"She does not date musicians! You're horrible, horrible people!" I say, laughing. "See you guys soon."

I head over to Times Square, feeling a nervousness in my stomach. I scan the street and spot a band from Ecuador playing some amazing flute music. I ask them if they know James. One of them says, "Yes. We've heard he is in the subways!" I thank them and break into a half-run toward the subway entrance; I'm two blocks away. I feel my Wolf-Sister flash up inside me; she will do this once in a while when I run and also when she vibes I need help. I'm peering out of her eyes now and sense my whole body breathing from head to foot as a wolf does. I have shape-shifted; I'm inside her spirit now. Sometimes I do this of my own volition, and sometimes she initiates it.

I can't get to the entrance soon enough. As I see the subway stairs up ahead, I'm thinking to myself, *What's going on with me? Why am I so nervous? It's not like me.*

When I get there, I flow down the steps, weaving around pedestrians, my Wolf's giant paws guiding me, smoothly, gracefully. Thankfully, I have a subway token and go quickly through the turnstiles. I stop and look around, wondering which way to go; it's like a maze down here. I close my eyes, go very still, and call to my Wolf-Sister, "Can you hear him, my Sister?" I feel her extend her hearing out. I pick up the sound of subway cars pulling into the station, to the left and right of me. Then I hear it! The faintest sound of music in the distance, directly in front of me. I start to jog again. I swiftly descend with more speed than usual a set of stairs to a crowded subway platform, feeling my Sister's sure feet beneath me. I look through the crowds of people waiting for trains, and I try to see past them. The music is a little louder, still ahead of me somewhere. As the subway rumbles in, I quickly glide around people on the platform, not bumping into anyone. I'm fully inside the rhythm of my Wolf-Sister's breathing and strides. Two bodies – one breath.

I arrive at another flight of stairs, and now I can clearly hear an electric guitar. In a burst of speed, we run up the stairs. At the top, the guitar sound is more defined, and I hear a beating of something underneath it. I slow down, noticing how the sound echoes off the subway station walls. The guitar riffs seem to join with the rushing sound of the subway cars as they pull in and out

– it's like they are another instrument – enhancing the
charging, pounding sound of the guitar. I spot a crowd
of twenty people about a hundred feet in front of me.
The sound of the guitar is more pronounced now – it's
haunting, mysterious, heavy. I feel like my heart is going
to come out of my chest.

My Wolf and I quicken our pace, and though I strain
to see over the heads of the crowd, I still can't see him.
I reach the people at the back of the gathering and move
through them, gently trying to not be rude. I glimpse
someone playing guitar. I slide around the last people,
and then I'm standing six feet in front of the musicians.
OH MY GOD, I scream in my head! I cover my mouth
with my hand in disbelief. My Wolf-Sister lets out a big
howl, ARH-WOOOOOOOOOOO, which she will do
when she witnesses something that makes her heart soar.

I feel tears on my cheeks. This is James Ryder, Char!
I shout inside. What I see is a striking, slender man,
about 6'1", with long, dark-brown, wavy hair, blue eyes,
jeans with a silver concha belt, and an ocean blue-shirt.
He looks lost, oblivious to everyone around him as he
wails, completely out of control on his Fender Stratocaster; the music seems to be pouring out of his whole
being. It's like a wave of thunder, crashing over me. I see
his partner drumming on three pails – I have no idea
how he creates such a big sound. They both seem to be
in another world. I stand there, holding my breath, shaking my head in awe. I peer around, wondering if anyone

else is getting this – the crowd is mesmerized, and no one is even talking. When I turn back to him, he is looking directly at me. Our eyes lock. The sadness reflected in his gaze is so deep and strong, it seems he was born with it. I can intuit how he channels it directly into his guitar – a very difficult thing to do – Hendrix and Robert Johnson could do it. I've never heard the song he is playing and I wonder, Is it one of his own?

He finishes and stares down at his guitar as if disbelieving what just flowed out. The crowd applauds, and pretty much all of them drop money in his case. He nods and smiles his thanks, but to me, it looks like he's in shock. Suddenly, for the first time in my life, I don't know what to do. I stand there frozen. He swings the guitar strap from over his shoulder, nods at his drummer, then he looks over at me and smiles simply, shyly. I step forward, totally shell-shocked, having no idea what to say.

I sputter out, "Wow, you can really play!"

"Thanks," he says with a tone I don't expect – a kind gentleness. Then he says sheepishly, "I don't know, I just lost it there for a moment…"

I feel an immediate desire to help him, "It was amazing, like you and the guitar…" I try to indicate awkwardly with my hands the sense of oneness. "Sorry…" – I'm the one embarrassed now.

"I know what you mean," he says softly, peering into my eyes; I sense him feeling me. His blue eyes are the color of a crystal-clear mountain lake in Montana.

I reach out my hand, "I'm Char."

He takes my hand and says, "I'm James, nice to meet you." I can feel his hand vibrating with energy. I don't want to let go, but I do quickly so I don't seem weird.

I respond, "You, too." I wait a beat and ask, "How long have you've been playing?"

The sadness flashes in his eyes again and he says with a heaviness, "Seems a long time." Out of the corner of my eye, I catch his drummer starting to pack up, counting up the money.

"For me too…" I respond, hearing my voice match the weight of his response.

He questions me with a tilt of his head.

"Sorry," I say, "I guess I was just thinking about myself. When you care really deeply about something, more than anything, more than you can even put into words, it feels like you've been doing it forever. Am I making any sense? Wow, sorry. How did I get into this? Sorry…" I look down at the ground, trying to hide. I don't know what's going on with me.

"It's okay. No reason to be sorry," he says in a reassuring tone. "Makes perfect sense to me." James's face brightens with surprise, like I said something cool.

"Really?" I respond, glad he isn't running for the hills.

He simply nods, smiling at me, those blue eyes comforting me. We stand there staring at each for a long moment. I feel so immediately connected to him. I don't understand it. I'm getting nervous with this level of intimacy, and it does feel intimate – I hadn't expected this.

I try and break the vibe by getting back to business. "Do you have a CD out?"

"I thought about it but I'm not good enough for that." I can hear a subtle anger in his tone, his face losing its warmth.

I blurt out, "You're good enough!" I hear the aggressiveness of my voice and tell myself to chill out.

"Thanks, that means a lot. What kind of work do you do?"

Okay! I think, *Here is my opening!*

"Well, speaking of CDs, I'm in the music business." Immediate alarm flashes across his face. I add, hoping it will convince him I'm for real, "I'm a producer with R&R Records, maybe you heard of them?"

He ignores me and quickly starts packing up the rest of his equipment. I see the drummer about ten feet away, watching us with his arms folded across his chest. Something about his expression doesn't look good. Now, I start to get *alarmed!*

I say quickly to James, trying to keep the panic out of my voice, "Is everything okay?"

"Sorry, I got to get going," he tells me in a nervous voice. The drummer hands him his cut of the money and they nod at each other – some kind of knowing passing between them.

"Wait, I wanted..." I blurt out, trying to stop him.

He hurries off towards the subway stairs. I quickly turn to the drummer, hoping I can figure out fast what's happening. My whole body feels like it's shaking.

"Hi."

He just glares me, a surly expression on his face.

"You know James?" I ask. Then I think, *have I gone stupid? Of course, he knows him.*

"Yeah," he answers with an obvious hostility, as if I've said something terrible.

"He ran off so quickly. Can you tell me what's the matter?" The feeling of being rejected is rushing up in me, like someone just broke up with me.

"You with a record company?" He questions me like I work for something evil.

"Yes, I'm putting a band together." I try and sound upbeat, positive.

"Ain't no use, lady. He don't play with no one but me," he says with finality.

"What do you mean?"

He picks up his pails and puts his drumsticks inside them and stares at me with a fierce protectiveness., "Nobody's going to fool with his stuff, lady," he says, shooting me a look of disdain before walking off.

I yell, "Wait..." but he just keeps going. I look around, feeling lost, a little dizzy, and say out loud, "What the hell is going on here?"

CHAPTER ELEVEN
James Ryder

I grab the first subway uptown. Thankfully the car is empty, since I don't feel like being around a crowd. My guitar and amp are in front of me, protecting me. I feel dazed – from the Native woman who appeared out nowhere and then losing it in my playing. I couldn't stop it, one of my own songs just came rushing through, and then a producer showed up.

When I first came to New York, I tried to honor my dad's wishes and made the rounds to record companies – actually, it was just two. I can see the first one like it was yesterday: a plush office, gold records on the walls, me sitting across from an A&R executive, bad vibes coming off him as he sat behind his big desk, half-listening to my demo tape. The phone rings, he picks up, talks, laughing with the caller, my special music completely ignored. He hangs up, clicks the cassette off, and says rapidly, "Maybe there is something there, but it needs a lot of work. I can put you in touch with one of my top producers and we can make it more presentable."

It was as if someone punched me in the gut. I countered, trying to control myself, "Presentable! It's my..." I heard my own words and just shut down. I wasn't going to explain myself to him. I left and didn't speak to a living soul for a week. I felt gutted. Six months went by and again, my dad's wish motivated me to get back out there, so I tried again – and got almost the exact same response. That was when I told myself I was done – *never again*.

But there was something about that woman. *Char was her name,* I think, *Man, she had something...hard to put into words ...she felt real. I just knew she got me when I saw her watching me play. She seemed to understand me losing it. There was a fierceness in her whole physical presence – but it didn't feel aggressive, more protective...I don't know.* I stare down at the palm of the hand she shook, still sensing the intense vibration coming from her touch.

CHAPTER TWELVE
Char Montgomery

Feeling like a lost child, I head back to the office because I can't think of what else to do. I blow by Annie and wave halfheartedly. I guess my face doesn't look too good because she asks me if I'm okay. When I see Red at the desk in front of my office, I can feel something in me start to break, and I try to rush past her.

Red asks, "Did you find him?" The happy expectation in her voice throws me over the edge and I feel the tears coming – I have no idea who I am right now. I shake my head and run into the office; she jumps up and comes after me.

"Red, please close the door," I implore her.

"Char, what's wrong?" she asks, alarmed.

I turn around, just staring at her as if I've been in an accident. I collapse on the old brown leather couch, another piece from home. She sits down next to me, waiting for me to speak, but I can't find the words.

"Char, you're scaring me, what's going on?"

I glance down at my cowboy boots, which always remind me of my roots. "I found him, Red, I found him."

I push the words out, a wave of uncontrollable emotion right behind them trying to break through – I try to pull it together.

"Awesome! So, what's the matter?"

I hold my head between my hands, trying to understand. "I don't know what happened. We were talking, really connecting. I was kind of an idiot, awkward. But it was okay, then I told him who I was, a producer, and suddenly he's splitting. His partner, this black kid who plays with him, he says he's the only one he plays with, and no one is going to mess with his stuff, and then he stomps off."

"Maybe it's not meant to be," Red suggests, always the cooler head.

"Red…" I stop, trying to find the right words so she will truly understand. "I have never heard anything like the sound that came out of this guy – never." I can feel the tears start to come again. "Look at me! What's wrong with me? Look, my hands are shaking." I stick my hands out to show her.

"I've heard stories about him," Red confirms with an ominous tone.

"It was like…" I search my heart for the words. "…his music reached inside me and touched something I didn't even know was there." I try to understand, to articulate it – "it touched the history inside me. I don't know. All is I know is that sound I've been searching for was six feet away from me, and I blew it…I blew it, Red..

I messed up."

Like a shot, Red jumps up and plants herself across from me; she doesn't look happy. She studies me – hard, with an ugly look on her face. Then she starts to search around the room, her eyes trying to find something.

"What are you doing?" I ask, confused.

On the edge of anger, with her hands on her hips, she yells, "What I'm doing?! I'm looking for Char Montgomery! She seems to have left the building."

Her confrontation has its effect and makes me realize I'm indulging in a pity party. I stare at her, fearing what she will say next. Then, with those emerald-green eyes blazing at me, she says, "I sit out at that desk and guard the gate because you are the finest woman I know. Period. You simply don't give up." She takes a breath and gazes around at the pictures on the walls, stopping at my favorite of a gorgeous black wolf with amber eyes, peering out between two trees as if she's playing hide-and-seek. Red amps up for a second assault, loving but tough. "Remember when I first came to work for you and asked you what all the wolves were about – especially that one with the amber eyes?" She points with one perfectly manicured red nail. Then, imitating my Western accent perfectly, she says, "'Red, that wolf there is me.' You jabbed your finger into your chest a couple times to show me. Then, you said in that hard bronc-riding cowgirl voice of yours, 'For me, she's saying, I'm here... here. You might not see me, but I'm here, and I have your back.' You remember?"

"I do, Red, I do." *Sometimes I've got be reminded*, I think.

"Good! Now, if you got your Char back together," she says giving me the smile that melts everyone and makes me laugh now, "I got something to tell you. You know that thing you've been asking me to find for a few months?" she asks, her face lighting up like she's got a cool secret.

"What thing?"

She pulls a piece of paper out of her blouse pocket like she is performing a magic trick and announces, "James Ryder's phone number and address!"

"What!" I grab it, reading it, thinking she's making it up. "You found it!"

"I had a good teacher," she declares, lacing her thumbs in her front jean pockets, mimicking every good cowgirl's pose, throwing in the curled lip of confidence.

I grab her in a hug, twirling her around, and we laugh like two teenagers. "Thank you, Red, thank you!"

Then something dawns on me, "Oh shit!"

"What's wrong?"

"I mean, I just couldn't call him up after what happened. That's like weird, like some kind of stalking... right?"

Red's face hardens a little with purpose and she motions with her chin over at my wolf photographs to remind me of the answer. Suddenly, my Wolf-Sister materializes out of the Dreamweave and stares at me, her eyes glowing with fierceness like two amber diamonds. I hear her voice – *"We are the sisterhood of the wolf – we never give up!"*

CHAPTER THIRTEEN
James Ryder

I hurry up the stairs to my apartment and discover Robert sitting on the floor against my door with his electric guitar and a perfectly contrived anger etched across his ten-year-old face.

I know he's not really upset, but I quickly say, "Sorry I'm late, pal. I took a walk after I finished." I hate being late for him.

"That's okay, me and the cock-a-roaches were becoming pals."

I laugh. "Come on, let's go in."

Robert bounces in, immediately plugs into an amp, swings his guitar into position, roots himself in his usual spot, and blurts out, "I'm ready!"

"Hey, give me a chance to figure out where I am!" I busy myself around my room for a minute, not really doing anything, feeling kind of out of it.

Robert slings his guitar to his side and reads me too well. "Did the cops hassle you again?"

"No, no, they're into it now." I sit down on the edge of my bed, that familiar feeling of disappointment swooping down on me; I wonder if I should tell him that it would be better if we practice tomorrow, as I don't want him to witness me in this state. He's watching me closely with that deep intuition of his; I know when he drops into that place.

"My dad called today," he reports.

This gets my attention. "Hey, great! How's he doing?"

"All right," he says half-heartedly, his eyes clouding over.

"What did you guys talk about?" I ask brightly, trying to hide the suspicion I feel from creeping into my voice.

"Well, he couldn't talk long, he's real busy with important stuff. He said he couldn't make it Saturday, but he'll definitely make it next weekend." I can see him trying to hold back the tears.

I check my anger and take an upbeat approach, "Okay, that gives us time to really practice so when you see him you can blow him away. I thought we'd start working on some Zeppelin."

His eyes widen and, surprised, he says, "Really! You think I can do it?"

"Absolutely, partner!" I confirm, giving him my most confident smile.

The phone rings, which is unusual; it barely rings. Robert has never heard the phone ring in my apartment. I ignore it, thinking it's probably a wrong number. Robert watches curiously, wondering what I will do. The caller doesn't relent, so I finally pick up and say tentatively into the receiver like it's some kind of bad news coming, "Hello."

"Hi, this is Char. Do you remember me? We met this afternoon."

I'm so stunned, I go mute.

"James?" she asks, checking if I'm still on the line.

"How did you get my number?" I confront her, stumbling for some reaction, and end up going with aggressiveness. I glance over at Robert, who's listening with eyes going wide, like he's witnessing a space ship landing.

Then she says with such vulnerability that it's hard for me to not listen, "James, I'm sorry for calling, for intruding. I don't know what I did to make you leave today, but is there any way we could talk?"

I'm frozen. Scared. I check Robert again; I can see him reading me, and the concern on his face tells me he hasn't experienced me this off-center before.

She adds, "I'm in your neighborhood. Could I come up and talk just for a few minutes, just a few minutes?"

She's in the neighborhood? I think, starting to freak out.

"You want to come up here?" I ask, alarmed at the prospect of anyone coming into my private space.

"Great! I'll be right up," she exclaims, super-excited.

"No, wait!" I hear the phone disconnect. I stare at the receiver in my hand, then look aimlessly around the room. I register the fire escape through the window and think, *I could get down it quickly.* Then I remember

Robert – he's staring at me, still trying to absorb that I'm going out of control, and he's not sure what to do. I feel myself start to panic.

"Hey, listen, there's a lady coming up here," I tell him, calming my voice, like it's no big deal.

"Can I stay?" he asks hopefully.

"It's business, you know?"

"Is it one of those record producers?" He asks with disdain, having heard some of my stories.

"Yeah."

"But aren't I your backup?" I can hear the disappointment lining his voice.

"Of course, partner," I reassure him.

Suddenly, there's a gentle knock on the door – but the sound of it feels like an explosion going off in the small room. We both freeze, staring at the wood door.

"James, it's Char," she announces softly through the door.

What's with this woman? I think, getting irritated. *Did she run here? But that tone in her voice – there is something about it – familiar.*

"James, I'm really sorry to barge in on you like this. Could we talk for a couple of minutes? Just a couple of minutes." Her voice just hangs in the air; the humbleness of it pierces through my walls and fear, and I decide to let her in. I take a big breath and open the door. Robert scoots behind me, hiding himself.

She stands there not saying anything, looking super-nervous; I immediately feel bad that I have made her feel this way with my abrupt manner. I didn't notice in the subway how naturally beautiful and unusual-looking she is. Before, her dark-brown hair was in a neat braided ponytail; now, it's shooting in all directions in thick lustrous waves, hanging down below her shoulder-blades – like she's some wild mountain-child that grew up with wolves.

"Hi," she greets me, timidly. She stays on the other side of the door, and asks, "Is it okay if I come in?" Her light amber-brown eyes seem very dark with feeling – serious. I wonder if she's been crying.

I can't get words out of my mouth, and so instead I just nod, backing up to let her in. Robert backs up, too, remaining hidden behind me.

As she walks in, she looks directly in my eyes and says, "I just want to apologize…" Then suddenly she stops when my room comes into full view. Her face flushes with emotion and, trance-like, she gazes slowly around, taking in all my vintage posters reflecting the history of early hard rock. I can see her energy slow down, her eyes sparkle like she has discovered a secret hideaway with countless treasures.

She steps reverently in front of my Hendrix poster advertising his concert at the Filmore and touches its surface with the utmost care.

I stand there very erect, my whole body alive with feeling at the way she honors my space. My eyes well up, a fierce pride flowing up in me.

She continues to explore the many posters, Zeppelin, Cream, Bind Faith, Woodstock. When she notices the picture of me and my dad, something unknown passes across her face. Her body has rotated fully around, her Spirit absorbing every part of my sanctuary, and then she rests her eyes on me, still standing by the open door. We don't say anything as the room vibrates with energy. I feel like I'm looking at myself, at my own soul, and I sense Robert peek around to glimpse at Char.

Surprised, Chars asks him, "Who are you?"

Robert steps from behind me and says proudly, "I'm Robert, James's backup guitarist! I live next store with my mom." No shyness in this kid!

"I'm Char, how do you do? Wow, you play guitar?!"

"Definitely!" he says, beaming at her.

"Would you play something for me?" A wonderful child-like innocence floats off her. I can see from the way she focuses on Robert, she is totally sincere and curious about him.

Excited, Robert looks up at me for permission. I smile and nod my head. He grabs his guitar, stands in his usual spot, and without hesitation or warm-up, plays a series of Hendrix riffs perfectly. The kid just has such confidence – no fear. I admire him for it.

Char applauds with great enthusiasm. Robert's eyes meet mine, checking for my approval, and I raise my fist in front of my chest in our traditional salute.

"If I didn't know it, I would've thought it was Jimi Hendrix himself!" Char proclaims.

"Really!?" says Robert. You could knock him over with a feather.

Char gives him a thumbs-up. "Absolutely!"

"You listen to Hendrix?" he asks, as if saying, *is it possible she could be that cool?*

"All day and all night!" Char confirms, laughing.

"I guess you don't have a mom then," he quips.

"Have you ever been to a rock concert?" Char asks him. There is a level of authenticity about her that I haven't seen that much in my life, or maybe I don't let myself see it in others, since very few people get through my barriers.

"No, James said he'd take me when I get older."

"Could I come?" She inquires, playfully hopeful.

"Can you get orchestra seats?" he asks.

"What!" I blurt out.

"Sorry, only kidding," Robert says.

"What grade are you in?"

"Fourth."

"I bet you have a lot of girlfriends."

"Why, you want to go out with me?" he fires back.

"I don't know…" Her beautiful face considers his proposal seriously. "…I don't usually date guitar players."

I admire the way she connects with my partner.

"But we're very cool!" He says, offering up the perfect argument.

I say, "Okay, I think it's time to turn in your guitar and do some homework."

"Okay," he says reluctantly and then turns to Char. "I'm doing a book report on Jimi."

"Awesome!" Char replies, her eyes lighting up. I like how passionate she is, and that she's not inhibited about showing it.

Robert lowers his voice as if he's sharing a secret. "Did you know Jimi's grandmother was a Cherokee Indian?"

"Yes, I did. I know she inspired the way he dressed."

"You mean the cool scarves and coats and stuff like that?"

"You got it."

"Say goodnight to Char," I tell him, firmly.

"Night! You listen to Hendrix all day and all night?" he asks to confirm this impossibility.

"I know! Incredible, right? Goodnight, James's backup."

"See you tomorrow, partner."

Robert leaves, holding his guitar protectively against his chest. I have never seen him happier.

CHAPTER FOURTEEN
James Ryder

He's very special," Char says. I notice she seems nervous after Robert leaves.

"I don't know what I'd do without him." I invite her to have a seat. Char sits down, taking a moment to study my room again as if she wants to get to *really* know me.

She starts to share a story as her eyes scan the collage of posters; there's a wistful tone to her voice. "When I was growing up, I'd sit with my older brother, Caleb, in his room, and we'd listen to the old groups for hours and hours." I pick up the Western accent, wondering where she is from. "Mountain, Jefferson Airplane, Janis, Blind Faith, Argent. He told me that music was a reflection of how he felt inside. The music was like his friend." She hesitates a moment, then says, "He was killed in Vietnam."

"I'm so sorry." My dad had great respect for Vietnam veterans; he felt they got a raw deal when they came home. A handful of veterans worked for him on the line at GM. He told me nobody was going to mess with them on his watch. When I would run into them, they all said the same thing, "Boy, your father has my back, that means something in this world – don't forget it." They all turned out for his funeral. The line of cars behind the hearse went on and on.

"Thank you. I don't why I brought that up – sorry. I seem to do that with you a lot!" she says, a big smile brightening up her face. The more I sit with her, the more I see her beauty could fool you; there is a hard-tough gleam that flashes up in her eyes periodically. I think to myself, *This is a person you could count on.*

"I'm honored," I say, hoping she knows I mean it.

We stare at each other, that intimacy I experienced in the subway station reigniting itself.

She spots my acoustic guitar. "That's a beautiful guitar." There is something about this woman's presence – she seems to *feel* everything.

"Thank you." I hesitate a beat, wanting to share something personal, which is not like me. "Sometimes I look at this guitar and it seems so vulnerable, you know? But at the same time, it's full of this force – this power. I can see the stories in it, all the great guitarists who played it. It just sits there, silent, waiting for me to pick it up. I put the strap over my shoulder, and something inside of me changes. I become a part of it. Even when I'm not holding it, I can feel it talking to me."

"What does it say?" she asks gently, her eyes filled with deep caring about what I might say. I'm blown away that she would think to ask that question.

"It's more like a feeling…a feeling of sadness…" I struggle, searching for the words. "I don't know. There's a communication there…"

"Does it feel like it's about other people?" she asks.

That surprises me. "I never thought about it like that."

"Sometimes when I listen to music, it's like there is something out there and I just can't…"

I finish her sentence. "…can't reach it, like it's calling you?"

"Wow, that's exactly right!" Her expression sparkles with happiness.

"Can I ask what got you into the music business?"

"This," she points to the posters. "I wanted to bring back the feeling that these groups had. It felt real, authentic, from the Spirit."

Everything she is saying is like an electric current that is connected to my heart. "So, you're looking for a guitarist?" I ask with a confidence and openness in my tone that surprises me.

"You guessed that, huh?" she says, a little embarrassed, grinning, her dark-brown, crazy thick hair falling over her face as she looks down.

I make an immediate decision and say, "Well, listen, I have been working on a couple things. Maybe you can check them out." I get up to find some tapes for her.

"Great! But I tell you what, why don't I get the other bands members together, and you can come in and meet the guys, and we can all listen together?"

"The band?" I ask, feeling the fear fire off in me.

"Yeah, I found these three incredible musicians – the very best. You will really like them. They're cool. How about tomorrow morning?"

"Tomorrow?" The anxiety of being judged slams into me.

"Sure. Is that okay?"

I stand up and pace the small the room.

"Come on, Char, I'm just some guy who plays on the street. These musicians you're talking about sound like professionals. I'm not in their league."

"James, if I say you're in their league, you are. You have a great gift. Don't turn your back on it."

I snap at her, "I'm not turning my back on anyone!"

"I didn't mean it like that," She says quickly, concerned I'm offended.

"I'm just not willing to put up with the nonsense of chasing a dream. Or of having people judging me."

"You can't stay in limbo forever. I don't understand why you've given up."

"Given up! Look, Char, I really appreciate you stopping by…" I feel my voice raising and can't seem to control it.

She starts to panic, scramble. "No wait, James, please don't push me away. I've waited a long time for this. You have that feeling, that sound I have been searching for. I'm so excited. Don't you know how special your playing is? It has nothing to do with techniques or speed or any of that other bullshit people think is important. You care so much, I can see it in you. Let me try to help you. The music is like your best friend in the world. A friend you would die for…"

I yell, "He already died!"

"What? What do you mean?"

"Look, I'm sorry…sorry for yelling at you." I hesitate a moment, feeling the gate shut inside me – again. "Listen, you just have to go. I'm sorry." I get up to move towards the door.

Then she says with such genuine caring, "James, please let me talk to you, please let me help you. I know you have turned a lot of people down. I know there are some real jerks in this business." The desperate expression on her strong pretty face is like a knife in me.

I feel like everything is crushing in on me. "Stop it, all right? Just let me be!" I open the door.

"Can't we…"

I step on her words, "…Don't you hear me now?" When I experience that ugliness come out of my mouth, I feel sick.

This beautiful, special woman stands frozen in front of me, her eyes filling with tears, staring at me in disbelief.

"Please go!" I implore her. She runs into the hallway, and I close the door behind her, feeling like I'm closing the door to my dreams. I listen to her run down the stairs, her steps becoming fainter and fainter. I have no idea why I'm acting like this. I realize in this moment, it's not really about my fear of what people or other musicians think of my music but something else that puts up a wall between me and the rest of the world – I scream inside my head, *WHAT'S WRONG WITH ME?* I sit on the edge of my bed, resting my elbows on my knees, holding my face in hands, shaking my head back and forth. "What is it?" I plead out loud to myself.

An anger starts to build inside me...an imaginary guitar fills my hands...my body moves to a familiar tempo, growing more intense until I jump up and, with great care, pull out a plastic-encased Jimi Hendrix album from my box of records. I set it up on the phonograph and pick up my electric guitar. Out of the speaker comes Hendrix's infamous "Purple Haze." I start to play in sync with the album. This is a ritual since I discovered Hendrix when I was a teenager; it always seems to ease my Spirit as I link up with his energy. I move the guitar and my body in rhythm with the pounding tempo, moving my fingers over the strings, finding the right positions innately. The song finishes but, on this day, my precious ritual doesn't seem to help me – I feel emotionally wasted. I gaze around my room, which usually keeps me safe from the outside world, but now a deep sadness permeates the air. Exhausted, I lie down on the bed, propping my head up with pillows, resting my guitar next to me. I pick up the picture of me and my dad standing next to his black Corvette and study the image, trying to project myself into that moment with him so I can feel his support. I miss him so much. I feel my eyes closing, grateful for the escape of sleep.

I'm dreaming now, thrust into the hospital room where my father lies, so small and fragile in the bed. He has been in and out of this hospital for two years, fighting cancer.

I'm holding his hand like a life-line, telling him, "Dad, what about that road-trip? We could go together." Then the hospital room dissolves into my nightmare: I hear Hendrix's song, "Are You Experienced." The psychedelic images of the video and his heavy guitar sound start crashing in on me, trying to open that door again, and suddenly I'm standing in front of the shack with the seven wooden chairs – empty. The same feeling – I sense them waiting, but for who? Then I'm quickly running, feeling someone next to me, but I can't move my head to see them...a gunshot...the sensation of something passing my ear, and then I'm back in the hospital room, my dad pulling me closer, ruffling my hair and whispering, "Never forget where you came from, son." His voice is so clear and present it wakes me up, as if he's here with me. I realize I'm in my apartment room and he's not alive but dead – it's like he died all over again. Wanting to snap out of this horrifying feeling, I sit upright and shake my head, shouting, "Why?" I see the record skipping on the turntable. Not able to hold the pain back any longer, I yell out loud, "Why? Why?"

Something snaps in me, and I swing at the turntable arm in anger, missing it, which ignites the buried rage inside me like a brush-fire, and I jump up and kick the crate of records – causing the phonograph to land flat on the floor; the Hendrix album is undamaged, but my other records are scattered everywhere. Suddenly, I'm out of control, as all the years of frustration and self-hatred pour out of me, and I start throwing my records around the room and ripping my cherished posters off the walls. I tear my Zeppelin and Hendrix music books to shreds. The madness has me in its grip, and I scour the room, searching for other pieces of my life to destroy – I spot my electric guitar, grabbing the neck and lifting it over my head to smash it, then suddenly the tears come in an uncontrollable rush, and I drop to my knees, sobbing, holding my guitar, my brother, protectively against my chest. "I'm sorry, I'm sorry," I cry to him. I fall back against the bed-frame, trying to catch my breath. Then, amidst the wreckage on the floor, I notice the framed picture of me and my dad. I clear the debris away and pick up the photo, staring hard at my dad's face, feeling his Spirit, his belief in me. I close my eyes, and a strong energy flows into me as I sense his arm around my shoulders again. I open my eyes, feeling my face harden with determination, and I make an enormous decision. I turn the frame over in my hands, opening the back – inside is a small white envelope. I hold it

in between the fingers of both hands, the tips of my fingers vibrating with what's inside. I repeat out loud,
"Okay, okay," my voice filled with gratitude. Carefully,
I tear open the envelope flap, reach inside, and take out
a set of shiny keys –the silver of the metal seems fresh
and clean and, most of all, new.

CHAPTER FIFTEEN
James Ryder

The taxi driver pulls up to a nondescript red-brick building in Queens. I feel good butterflies inside me, an excitement; I pay him, giving him a big tip because it just feels right in this special moment. I exit the taxi very slowly as a way of honoring this place. In front of me is a dark red garage door – there is no one on the street. That familiar, beautiful stillness I feel when I play guitar flows up inside me. I pause, letting my soul sense what's waiting for me inside the garage. After a minute, my instinct tells me the time has arrived, and I unlock the garage door, pushing it up until it's fully open.

The garage is pitch black; I turn on the overhead light, revealing a large shape covered by a heavy, black tarp that almost fills the entire length of the dusty room. I chuckle, experiencing a teenage rush of excitement – what's hiding underneath the tarp is "the ultimate coolness." I carefully pull back the cover to reveal a black '67 Corvette in perfect condition. A big smile stretches across my face as I admire the beautiful car and remember my father. I reach out and touch the glossy fender, reintroducing myself. "I'm finally here, pal. Are you ready!"

CHAPTER SIXTEEN
James Ryder

I stand over Robert, watching him sleep peacefully with his arm curled around his guitar, holding it close. *What a gift he has been to me,* I think. I take a moment to memorize his face so I can keep his spirit with me on my journey. Then, very quietly so as not to wake him, I place my plastic-encased Hendrix album with a note attached on his nightstand and give him our fist-salute, whispering, "I will see you soon, partner. Count on it."

CHAPTER SEVENTEEN

James Ryder

I'm behind the wheel of the Corvette, speeding through the empty, garbage-can-lined streets of Manhattan, watched over by stray dogs and decaying tenements. I go over in my head what I wrote Robert in the note I left him:

> *Dear Backup, Your guitar looked like it needed some rest, so I didn't wake you. As you're reading this note, I'm flying down the highway on that road trip my dad wanted me to take. It's important for you to know I wish I could take you with me, but this is something I need to do alone. Maybe there are some answers out there for me. I know you'll understand this – you're really smart. Here's my Hendrix album, you hold onto it for me, okay? Don't forget to keep practicing. I know you won't. I'll be back, you have my word. Take good care of your mom, and keep it below concert level.*
>
> *Love, James*

I pull onto the highway, shift gears, and as I accelerate

past slower cars, I enjoy the roar of the Corvette's engine. Within minutes, I'm crossing the George Washington Bridge. I turn my head for a last glimpse at the city – the skyscrapers are ablaze in the dawn light, wishing me well, and I sense the *rightness* of my decision to go. I like this new feeling.

CHAPTER EIGHTEEN
James Ryder

Hours later, I peer through the windshield as I pass a fluorescent green sign: *Ohio*. Thick forests loom up on both sides of the three-lane highway, and the road is empty, which feels freeing. My dad left a good assortment of eight-tracks for me, having customized the stereo to play them. It's the only thing that isn't stock; he was kooky about everything being stock – he was a GM guy! I'm listening to "Hold Your Head Up" by Argent. Love this song! It feels appropriate to the start of my adventure. The Corvette is so powerful, I must keep watching my speed. It's good to be out of the city concrete and to feel some trees around me – something inside me relaxes. The unfamiliar pleasure of it surprises me. I glance at my dad's Rand McNally Road Atlas laying on the passenger seat – knowing it was his feels comforting. I rest my body deeper into the black leather bucket seat. I have no idea where I'm going. I've been driving for eight hours and decide to call it a day, so I get off the next exit and follow the signs indicating: *Motel*. After fifteen minutes and a lot of turns, it feels like I'm heading in the wrong direction, going further from a town. I haven't passed another car in a while.

Suddenly, up ahead on the left, I notice a red glow in the night. My speed rushes me towards whatever it is, and within less than a minute, I register it's a sizable fire on the side of the road. I immediately take my foot off the accelerator to slow my speed. It's a tractor-trailer that has crashed into what looks to be an above-the-ground small fuel tank; the woods next to the truck are on fire. The nose of the hood is crushed but the trailer itself seems to be intact. There are no emergency vehicles, so it must have just happened. I slow even more, and as I pass, I focus my vision and catch sight of a man's head above the passenger window in the truck cab. "Oh, shit," I say, slamming hard on the brakes. The Corvette screeches, and its rear-end fishtails fifty feet across the blacktop. I keep cool and steer it under control, drive onto the shoulder, jump out, and sprint towards the truck. I quickly assess the fire is still at a safe distance but creeping closer to the cab. I get up on the step below the passenger window and peer inside and find a tough-looking man in his late forties, unshaven, lying unconscious; his head is bleeding but not too bad. I pull on the handle to open the truck door – it's jammed. I make another attempt – no luck. I bang on the passenger window repeatedly, trying to wake him – nothing; he's out cold.

I observe the flames are reaching higher, growing

stronger. I figure I only have a few minutes to get him out. I decide to try the door again, shifting my weight to get better leverage. My arms strain, pulling at the door – it won't budge. *Maybe the other side*, I think, and run around to the driver's side where I find a tree wedged up against the door. I conclude right away the tree is too heavy to move. I glance down the road – "Where are the cops?" I wonder out loud in frustration. I feel panic out there on the edges, and I decide to bang on the windshield in front of the driver, hoping a different angle might rouse him. By the growing roar of the flames behind me, I know the fire is closer; smoke is starting to get in my eyes. I bang harder. The man finally stirs, slowly regaining consciousness, and realizes where he is. He spots me through the glass, eyes wide in alarm.

Relieved, I yell through the window, "Your truck is on fire! Got to get you out! Door jammed."

He shouts in a husky voice, "Okay," accepting what needs to be done. He's dazed, but alert.

Then I have a bright thought and call to him, "What's your name?"

"Jake," he responds.

"I'm James." He gives me the thumbs-up and makes an effort to clear his head by sitting up and rubbing his face. He notices the blood but doesn't freak out.

I ask him, "Can you push on your side?"

He does another thumbs-up and positions his feet on the door as I ready myself to pull from my side.

Coughing from the smoke, which is getting denser, I give him the count of three and yell, "Go!" We both strain with effort on either side. The door gives a little.

"One more time," I encourage him.

Jake makes the "okay" sign with his thumb and index finger, and we give it another big push/pull – still nothing.

"Dammit!" I scream. I can feel the heat from the blaze on my face; I take a fast scan around and see we're rapidly running out of time. The fire is burning through the grass, thirty feet from the truck's gas tank. I get Jake's attention and holler at him, "JAKE, I WILL GET YOU OUT!"

He points in front of him, telling me, "The windshield, smash the windshield!"

"Okay. Find something to cover yourself up with." He shields himself with a blanket from the sleeper behind him.

I climb on top of the hood and kick the glass and almost fall off the truck! I try again, kicking from the side, but the glass doesn't relent. I yell into Jake, "It won't work. Can you try it?"

He shouts, "Okay, get out of the way." I leap off the hood – praying this will work. I turn around, seeing the fire is now twenty feet from the gas tank, shrinking the open area around the truck. The windshield moves in its frame, once, twice, then nothing. I jump up to see what's happening – Jake is passed out!

"Oh fuck!" I yell. An unfamiliar steely resilience grabs hold of me, and I roar at the flames, "NO FUCKING WAY!"

I feel my eyes harden in anger and I spin around, searching the area in front of me for something to smash the window and retrieve a sizable branch. I charge up the truck hood, position my feet so my stance is secure and hit the glass with all my strength – it cracks!

"ALL RIGHT!" I shout. Then, in a frenzy, I come down on the glass over and over again, shattering it in large chucks. I quickly peel the windshield back with the branch, reach in, and shake Jake back to consciousness. "Jake, can you make it?" He moves his head up and down rapidly to show me he's up for it.

I step through the demolished windshield very carefully and hold onto Jake as he navigates over the glass. We slide down the hood together, me holding him by the belt. I sense by the intense heat on my back, we're almost out of time. When I turn around, the flames seem to be trapping us on all sides – a wave of fear rushes up in me. I peer through the smoke, searching for a way through, and spot a narrow, open corridor to the treeline – the flames flicker across the opening – it's not perfect, but I don't see any other choice.

I grab Jake under the arm and point to the opening, which is closing rapidly. I yell, "We have to give it a try."

He nods, his face grave but determined, and shouts, "FUCK IT!" We sprint though the corridor between the flames to a safe distance in the trees, just missing the flames trying to reach out and get us. Suddenly, the gas tank explodes, knocking us off our feet. Jake screams, "Incoming!" and crawls frantically behind a tree. I scramble fast after him and grab his shoulders, guiding him to sit against the tree. He stares at me, eyes wide in fear. I know exactly what his scream means – Jake is a Vietnam vet.

With fierce intensity, I shout, "Jake, you're home... you're home."

He registers my voice and the word "home" and looks at me in desperation, "I'm home?"

I will always remember the expression of fear on this toughened man's face. "Yes, you're safe, Jake," I reassure him, emphasizing his name to orientate him. As I look at him, I see he's filled with the same pain as the vets that worked with my dad – eyes that have "seen too much."

"Oh shit, I thought...Sorry," he says, embarrassed, lowering his head, shaking it back and forth.

"It's okay, man. You're *safe*," I tell him, quietly, hoping he hears in my voice that he is truly home and there is never a reason to be sorry for being afraid – never.

CHAPTER NINETEEN
James Ryder

At the Emergency Room, the nurse comes out and tells me I can visit Jake. I find him lying on a hospital gurney, holding a compress-bandage to his head. His rough, grizzled appearance and black, smoke-charred face stand out in contrast to the white sheets and antiseptic cleanliness of the ER. As I get closer, I can see he's okay but not happy with himself.

"Hey, Jake. How are you feeling?"

"All right. Just going to need a couple of stitches. James, right?"

I reach out my hand and say chuckling, "Nice to meet you," wanting to make light of the ordeal we just went though. The toughened skin of his grip reminds me of my dad's hands.

"I didn't get a chance to thank you for saving me out there."

"No problem," I respond, trying to brush it off.

With a firm voice, he counters, "No, James, you didn't give up...you could have been killed...I wouldn't have made it." The deep lines on his face harden, emphasizing his seriousness.

His words about being "killed" and the pronounced way he speaks my name sparks a dark, heavy emotion to rush up inside me that's out of sync with what he's just said. This is not the first time I've had this strange feeling – it's almost like a shadow in me that is blended with sadness and apprehension. I catch him watching me like he's seeing something in me that I don't know about myself.

I only feel capable of silently acknowledging Jake's appreciation. He glances around the ER, and I wonder if he's trying to fully absorb where he is; the room is quiet with only one other patient.

"This is the second bad accident in three years," he tells me. "My wife wants me to quit driving. She doesn't understand, I love to drive those trucks, to be on the road...I don't know...it feels..." His face breaks out in a little boy's ear-to-ear grin; it's startling how quickly it transforms his appearance. He continues, "...it just feels good, like an adventure. Is it worth my life? I don't know..."

He seems to contemplate his own question; I just stay still, listening keenly – I sense this man is talking from his soul and I want to honor its importance. Then he nods his head in acceptance and says, "Maybe it's worth the chance of dying to do something you love so much..." He looks directly at me, as if to share with another human his inner-world, and adds, "...I don't know, my new friend."

Suddenly, I feel dizzy, disoriented.

"You okay?" Jake asks, and his worry flashes me back to my Dad and how his concern made me feel stronger – I knew I wasn't alone.

"Yeah, sure, I guess just little wiped out."

"Understandable." He reaches out his hand again and I immediately grasp it; he looks hard in my eyes, squeezing my hand firmly, and says hoarsely, "James, I won't forget what you did…" He hesitates and turns his eyes away from mine, I think trying to push the emotion back. I'm glad, because I can feel myself getting choked up. "…I'm okay here. You get on down the road…" He studies my energy for a second and declares, "…you're one of us now."

I look at him questioningly, not understanding.

Jake adds as if to answer me, "When we were in-country, we counted on each other – it was the code. You understand, James?"

Pride surges up in me. My dad taught me the *way* – truly.

Chapter Twenty
Char Montgomery

Two days after James threw me out of his apartment, I'm standing in front of his building, trying to figure out what to say to him. I've barely slept. This is my second attempt to knock on his door, but at least this time I've gotten past the sidewalk. I guess I'm in full-blown stalking-mode now. I've worn my special deer-skin fringed jacket with bead-work on the back done by a Native friend to give me a connection to where I'm from. I need my roots now, and my Wolf-Sister stands beside me. Back at the office, she kept nudging me from behind with her nose to get my butt out the door. It wasn't the first time she had pushed me directly into fear. Even though she lives in the *Dreamweave*, I can definitely feel her physically, especially when we're out in the wilderness and I sense her brush against my leg – it's pretty wild. On the way over, I listened to Zeppelin's "Whole Lotta Love" on my Walkman to get me psyched. I'm calling in all my inspiration! The only real problem is I'm not sure if I'm here for the band or for James – if it's for James, then I may be in deeper trouble.

I have never felt this kind of instantaneous chemistry or connection with a man. I also don't want to live with the possibility of blowing things by letting my soulmate just brush by me. That's too enormous to even contemplate. I was less nervous sitting on a dangerous bronc in the chute at the rodeo when I was seventeen years old. Finally, I realize I'm going to make this right with him. So, I climb the steps of the brownstone and open the front door. I laugh to myself at the stories my friends used to tell back home when guys wanted to ask me out – they were all terrified! Now, it's my turn to experience this fear of rejection. Those poor cowboys – *I'm sorry, guys, you're getting your revenge now.* I stand by James's door and I actually feel a little sick, but I bite the bullet and knock. I wait fifteen seconds and try again. Oh, God, I wonder, would he actually be inside and not answer?

I speak in a tiny voice through the door, "James?" A mouse would be embarrassed at my timidity! Still no response. I knock again. "James, it's Char Montgomery..." I go for humor: "You know, Char, the Bigfoot monster you met the other day."

I conclude in my mind, *If he's not going to open the door, then I'll just say my piece here.* I lean my forehead against the door, hoping to communicate my soul through this barrier. "Listen, James, I just want to tell you how sorry I am about the other night. I know I was really pushy..." I stand there hoping with my whole being for a response. Even "Go away!" would be better than nothing.

I shake my head. Feeling defeated, I mutter, "...I just want to tell you I'm sorry. Okay..." I write a note, telling him the same thing, and slip it under his door, my ears on full-extension to see if I hear anything inside – not a peep. As I head down the hallway, passing another apartment door, I hear an electric guitar inside; I surmise this must be Robert's apartment. I hesitate a moment, but then I just leap from the cliff again like the crazy person I've become and knock.

"Who is it?" Robert asks with mock-suspicion from the other side of the door.

"It's Char, Robert, remember from the other night with James?"

Before I even finish speaking, he swings the door open and says excitedly, picking right up from where we left off the other day, "Hi, Char. I'm practicing, did you hear?"

"Yes! Sounds great!" I see his mother come from behind him and I say quickly, "Hi! Sorry to bother you."

"You're Char?" She asks, her eyes lighting up like I'm a long-lost relative. The enthusiastic way she greets me is like warm sunshine to my dark mood. *Maybe I'm not Bigfoot after all.*

"Yes!" I say.

As I reach out my hand, she opens her arms and says, "We're huggers here!" I don't think I have ever needed a hug more! Even though Joan is a tiny woman, her embrace feels like a giant warm blanket on a cold day.

"I'm Joan, come on in. All I've heard for two days is 'Char said I sound like Jimi!'"

I look down at Robert, "Absolutely!"

"You see, Mom!"

"I'm so sorry to bother you," I say, repeating myself and feeling bad that I'm involving these nice people in my relentless obsession. Their apartment is as neat as a pin and very homey.

Joan studies me, her brow furrowing, and asks, "Is everything okay, honey?"

I take a big breath, wanting to share with this kind woman what's happening. "I think I really upset James. I wanted him to join a special band I'm putting together. I was wondering if you've seen him?"

Robert says quickly, like it's not a big deal, "James left."

"He left? Where to?" I ask, pushing the panic down.

"Road trip," Robert says flatly, like he's reporting the news.

"Yes, he left two days ago pretty early in the morning," Joan confirms.

"Do you have any idea where he went?" I inquire, hoping she knows.

"No, he was just going…you know…" she says, waving her hands in the air to indicate he could be anywhere.

"Did he say when he'd be back?" I ask, looking for something to hang onto. I feel like I'm slowly drowning.

"No, I'm sorry," she responds, shaking her head as if she feels bad about disappointing me. She has the kindest eyes.

All the air goes out of me. Seeing my state, Joan invites me to sit down. She and Robert both watch me, looking startled, concerned. I feel terrible that I'm sitting in their cozy apartment having a total meltdown.

"You know, Char," I like the way Joan says my name – it feels like a happy name when she speaks it, "there's got to be a pony in here somewhere!"

I look at her confused.

"You never heard that story?"

I shake my head, feeling as if I've lost the will to speak.

Joan smiles and explains, "They took these two little boys and put one of them in a room full of these great toys and incredible candy and locked him in there for an hour. Well, they came back and opened the door, and there he was, sitting on this little stool, just sort of pouting, and nothing had been touched, and they asked him, 'How come?' He said that he figured he'd probably break something or eat too much candy and get sick, so he didn't touch anything. Well, they took the other little boy and put him in the room full of all this horse-manure. And they came back in an hour and there he was, with this little shovel and this big grin on his face, digging away, and they said, 'What are you doing?' and he replied, `Well, I figured that with all this horse manure, there must be a pony in here somewhere!'"

I laugh appreciatively and say to Joan, "How did you know a horse story would make me feel better?"

"You got the West written all over you!"

Joan is one of those special people who just intuit what you need.

Robert puts his arm around my shoulders and suggests, "You could use me in the band till he comes back!"

"You're available?"

"Absolutely! Let me show what I've been practicing!"

Chapter Twenty-One
James Ryder

I've been on the road four days now, growing used to the rhythm of motels, gas stops, and fast food places. Lots of cool reactions from folks about the Corvette. I stop at a railroad-crossing and just enjoy watching a long freight train pass by as I listen to "Ramble On" by Led Zeppelin. I'm finally "rambling on," and hearing the song makes me happy that I'm *actually* doing it. The dramatic encounter with Jake raised a few questions – some are clear, some not so much. A lot happened in such a brief moment. My dad would have liked Jake. The caboose motors by, revealing miles of golden wheat fields framed by a pale blue sky. Seeing this part of the country up close as opposed to in a movie makes a difference – the land is truly spectacular. When the wind passes over the wheat, it's like a golden wave. I want to pull over and run through the fields like a kid. I spot a sign ahead: *Lexington, Kentucky – 150 Miles.* I notice a young guy, probably in his mid-twenties, standing next to the sign, hitchhiking; he's tall with a proud bearing and short blond hair parted on the side. There's a worn suitcase, strapped with a belt, at his feet. I think to myself, *Why not?* and pull over on the shoulder next to him.

I call out, "Where you heading?"

"About ten miles up the road," he says brightly, his voice heavy with a Southern accent. As he gets closer to the car, I catch a deep tiredness around his eyes, unusual for someone that young. I motion with a wave and smile for him to jump in. As he does, I extend my hand and introduce myself; his name is John Cooper. Something about the way he immediately sits quietly in the passenger seat as I pull out on the road impresses me – I sense his politeness and an awareness that he's in my space.

"Thanks for stopping – much appreciated." The respectful quality in his voice feels Old World.

"Sure. Heading home?" I ask.

"Yeah, the family farm…" he says, a subtle hesitation in his tone as something shifts in his energy. "I noticed your plates. You're from New York?" I vibe he's deflecting me.

"Yeah," I answer, feeling my own little shift from his simple question. There is a heaviness back in New York that I'm happy to put behind me. It's only Char's hurt face that is hard to let go of. I feel terrible for the way I treated her. And there was an intense chemistry between us that I would be blind to deny.

"Ever been out in this part of the country?" John asks.

"No, but it seems familiar to me," I respond, not understanding why I would think that. Then I add,

"Maybe it's because I feel closer to the land out here – I sense my connection to it."

I feel John study me with a quick glance; something about what I said seems to have caught his attention. He looks in the back where my guitars are.

"You play guitar?" he asks, an out-of-place seriousness to the question.

I just nod at him. It feels difficult to acknowledge this for some reason; I've had four days to disconnect from this part of me.

As if reflecting on something he deeply misses, John says, "I grew up with a lot of music in the house. Been away from home for a while, singing at fairs, dances, bars."

"What was it like – singing on stage?" I ask him, sincerely interested. I feel John's eyes on me, surprised at that simple question.

He takes a moment to answer. "It felt like a different kind of home. Like I was doing something good, sharing something."

I acknowledge that I totally understand with a silent nod. You ever meet someone, and within a few minutes, you feel an unexplainable connection to him or her? That's what I'm experiencing.

"Where you heading?" he asks.

"Not really sure. Mississippi, maybe."

"The root of all of it is down there." I feel him wanting me to understand this as someone who plays guitar.

A sudden chill travels through my body, and that dark unknown energy feels present again.

"You mean music?" I ask, though a part of me fears even saying the words.

"Truly, James, truly." He taps his heart, and there's a *knowing* gleam in his eyes.

"My turn is right ahead." John points to a right turn, fifty yards away. I pick up a little nervousness in his voice.

"How long since you been home?" I ask him.

"Three months now." A weight in his tone again; he takes a big breath, seeming to release the tension.

I turn onto a narrow dirt road and come upon a classic American farm setting with a main house surrounded by support buildings and two silos, expansive fields of corn stalks all around the perimeter – it's like the buildings sit in an oasis surrounded by corn.

A hundred yards later, we pull up in front of a white colonial home fronted by a big porch and well-cared-for flower beds. John jumps out and yells up at the house, "Hey, I'm home!"

Suddenly, a family piles out the front door in an explosion of happiness. In that moment, I feel like the luckiest guy in the world to witness such joy. I see two teenage girls and a little boy and an older woman who I am sure is his mother. I get out of the Corvette and hang back as John runs to them and hugs the kids first, then hugs his mother who stares at his face, checking his emotional state. There is obviously a deep family love here.

I hear him say, "Come on, everyone, I want you to meet James. He gave me a ride from down the road." He calls out to me, "Hey, James, come meet my family."

As I amble towards the group, John says, "James, this is my mom, Kate."

"How do you do, ma'am?" I reach out to shake her hand, bowing my head respectfully in greeting. Kate is a pretty woman in her early fifties, with thick blonde hair tied back in a bun. What I notice is her quiet presence. Now I understand where John gets it from.

"Nice to meet you, James. Thanks for giving my boy a ride." She grasps my hand in both of hers for a long moment, making eye contact and then glancing over my shoulder at my car. She seems to receive something as she studies me and the Corvette as if she recognizes a young man's demons.

Then, with unexpected formality, John, introduces his siblings, and I get the sense of how important they are to him. "James, these are my two sisters, April and Laura, and my brother Joshua."

April looks to be eighteen years old with straight blonde hair down her back and a Deerfield baseball cap on her head; Laura, who is maybe two years younger, has darker blond hair in a pony tail and a no-nonsense look in her eyes; and Joshua, about eight years old, is bursting with excitement at seeing his brother. The energy at this farm feels charged. I have never seen teenagers or children stand with such pride. April takes off her cap, steps forward, and extends her hand with a solemn friendliness "Welcome," she says.

Then her younger sister Laura reaches out her hand to me, "Welcome to our home, James."

I'm a little blown away by their comportment. I feel emotion rushing up in me and try to pull it back.

Then Joshua runs up to me and tugs on my hand, "I'm Joshua!"

I squat down at his height and say, "You're John's older brother, right?" He's one of those kids you know is always exploring and having adventures – finding happiness along the way.

"I keep telling him that!" Joshua responds, laughing.

John says to his mother, "James is going to be staying for dinner." He glances over at me, catching my eye to ask if that's okay. I nod softly, smiling to let him know it's appreciated.

"Of course. We wouldn't have it any other way!" Kate declares.

CHAPTER TWENTY-TWO
James Ryder

Laughter fills the dining room of the Cooper house as everyone finishes the main course. I notice the array of family pictures on the walls. I see a strong-looking man in them who's obviously the father; he has thick hair, big shoulders like an ex-football player, and looks to be in his early fifties. I wonder where he is. The family is hanging on every word John says – he has been truly missed.

April, the older sister, who has been eyeing me every so often between bites of food, is getting me a little nervous. Finally, she asks me straight-out, with no warm up, "Do you have a girlfriend?"

John immediately intervenes, "Oh my God, he's only been here 15 minutes!"

April fires back, "What! You mean this isn't a set up like you used to do?

I catch Kate sitting back, enjoying the banter. Earlier, she kept running around the kitchen until John made her take the apron off and finally sit down.

"Set up!" John yells, aghast as such an accusation.

"No, I don't have a girlfriend," I say, smiling.

Laura, the younger sister, chimes in, "How come?" Like I said, she's no-nonsense!

"That's a good question," I reply. "I did meet someone back in New York just before I left. Pretty gorgeous, just like you two." Both girls turn beet-red.

Joshua adds, "I have a girlfriend!"

"Just one?" I ask, and we all laugh.

"We held hands," he says, just informing the table, not boasting.

"Wow!" John and I exclaim at the same time.

John teases Joshua, "When are you getting married?" I can see how much pleasure he takes in being home.

"Maybe in a few weeks!" Joshua tells us, giggling.

John turns to his mother, "You know, Mom, that's the best meal I think I've ever eaten, hands down.

"I cooked, and your father sang," Kate says, brightly.

In an instant, all the happiness leaves John's strong face, and he stares, frozen, at his mother. The kids look alarmed; the wonderful energy has gotten sucked out of the room.

"John, I'm…" his mother says quickly, a self-punishing, regretful tone in her voice. I'm not sure what's it's about.

John, who is not able to hold in what's going on inside him, hurriedly gets up and says, "Sorry…" and walks out of the dining room and out of the house. I hear the screen door banging behind him. The family stays quiet, seeming to understand what this all about.

Kate leans over to me and asks gently, "James, can you check on him?" The concern for her son is evident; she motions to the other kids with her hands to stay still. They don't move, trusting their mother's instinct to send me.

"Yes, ma'am." I walk out to the front yard and search for John. I hear a commotion in the corn field about a hundred yards to the right and jog towards it.

As I get closer, I hear John yelling, "NO, NO, NO!"

I discover him out of control, swinging at the corn stalks, and I yell out, "John! John, what's going on, man?"

He doesn't hear me, so I run up in front of him and see his face is streaming with tears.

"John, what's happening?"

He finally becomes aware of my presence and shouts, "He's gone…he's gone!"

He falls to his knees, trying to catch his breath. I get down on the ground close to him. I don't say anything, just wanting him to know I'm there.

Finally, he raises his head, looks in my eyes, and says, "My father is gone, James…he's dead." He puts his face in his hands, shaking his head in disbelief.

"Mine too, brother, mine too," I respond without thinking. I understand the disbelief of losing a father, you just *don't understand* they're gone – it doesn't make sense. He raises his eyes up at me, surprised, as if realizing he might not be alone in this suffering.

"Really?" This information seems to begin to settle

him down. "When did he pass?"

"About six years ago, when I was twenty-two."

"Wow, you were young."

"Yeah." I'm sure he can hear my sense of loss in my voice.

"Dad died three and a half months ago – heart attack. Two weeks after the funeral, I had to leave. I couldn't stand to be here without him. He was everything to me…everything. Maybe I came back too soon?"

"I don't know about that," I say gently.

John just looks at me questioningly with his red, tear-filled eyes.

I add, "You're needed here, brother."

John nods his head, seeming to absorb that simple fact at a deeper level.

I see him going somewhere in his thoughts, and then he shares with me, "Man, my dad could sing. He believed that music was a way of thanking God for all we have. We're mountain-people from way back, James – came down to farm when my dad was our age – the mines had played out." John takes a breath trying to calm himself further. He scoops up a handful of soil in his hand, feeling its texture. "He told me I have one of them mountain-voices from the old times – that the earth was in my voice…" Squeezing the dirt in his hand tightly, perhaps to lock his father's words even more fully inside, he repeats quietly to himself, "…The earth was in my voice…When I was up on stage, he was always out in the audience giving me that look of pride. He told me, 'I took him back home.'"

"I got to believe he's still out in that audience," I say reassuring him, and repeat inside myself, *the earth was in his voice* – what a beautiful expression – it knocks on some closed door deep inside me.

John looks over at the house, all lit up, the front yard sparkling with fireflies. I follow his gaze and suggest, "Looks like there is happiness over there."

"We've had a lot of good old times in that house, James," he tells me, his mood brightening.

"Well, I have my guitar with me," I throw out to him, hoping to be of some help to these special people.

"I was thinking of asking you, but maybe it's just too soon for them, for me."

I say from my heart, "I really wish I could have met your dad, John – truly. But you know what? I met *his son*." John studies me as if I just said something very important; his energy goes very still, then he looks down at the ground, seeming to want to absorb even deeper what he just heard. He nods his head up and down as if understanding something. Maybe it's the same thing I just heard: we are our fathers' sons – we are the embodiment of them – they are not lost or gone forever.

John lifts his face to me and I can see the beginning of hope in his eyes; he quickly reaches out and gives me an excepted hug and says, "Thanks for coming to find me."

CHAPTER TWENTY-THREE
James Ryder

The moonlit porch is filled with the voices of the Cooper family singing. I feel so grateful to accompany them with my guitar at this special time for them. Joshua has his own little guitar and plays along, reminding me of Robert, whom I wish was here to share this. I know he and Joshua would become fast buddies. It's good to get my acoustic guitar in my hands – he's my best friend, and it feels wonderful to share this moment with him. Like me, he wants to feel happy. We've had enough sadness.

"James, wow! You can play!" Kate says with exuberance, her wise face glowing.

"Thank you, ma'am," I say, shyly. Other than a compliment from my dad, this mother's praise means more than I can say. I see John squinting his eyes, studying me closely, that same look he gave me in the car – like he's *seeing* something. We catch each other's eye, and he nods as if to confirm what he suspected – though I'm not sure what that is.

"Joshua, that was really good!" I tell the young boy, not wanting him to feel left out.

"Really?" he asks, his eyes wide.

"Definitely!" I say.

"John, would you sing my favorite?" Kate asks, a little apprehensively.

"Oh, John, do it!" Aprils says, her voice pleading playfully.

"Do it a cappella, Johnny," Laura adds.

"Okay," John consents, seeing how much his mom wants this.

April and Laura, bundled up in sweaters, settle at their mother's feet as Joshua cuddles in her lap, a hand-woven blanket covering him.

John begins to sing Neil Young's "Old Man." I will tell you, brothers and sisters, I truly understand what his dad meant by *the* earth was in his voice – his singing is pure, raw, directly connected to his soul – each lyric he sings has a world of heartache behind it. Every hair on my body stands up, and I feel all my emotions come alive and my eyes well up. I have a vision of him up there in the Ozark Mountains in a cabin, singing on the porch in a voice that is unblemished by modern society – his voice is primitive, it is history. I have experienced the same feeling with only one person before – Robert Johnson, king of the Delta Blues, the iconic musician from the 1930s whose gritty, emotional vocals and other-worldly slide guitar influenced many rock legends, including Eric Clapton, Led Zeppelin, The Rolling Stones, and Bob Dylan. In the middle of the song, John motions for me to join in. I've never sung with anyone in my life other than with my dad. I worry that I'm intruding on the family's request and look quickly at his mother who, sensing my insecurity, urges me to go ahead with her eyes. *Okay,* I think, and join John on the chorus. I have no idea how it happens, but John and I are immediately in perfect harmony. But there is also something more - a rich, lush, tonal quality in the sound of our joined voices. We look at each other, kind of blown away. Connecting like this with another singer feels so joyful. I had no idea you could have this sense of oneness. And to sing a song about fathers with another vocalist who also lost his father – no words, brothers and sisters.

I glance over at his family, who are all suddenly sitting up very straight, listening in a very different way than they were a moment ago. Especially April, whose face seems focused and serious as if she can't quite believe what she is hearing. We come to the end of the song and John and I just stare blankly at each other, both of us disbelieving what has just happened. I'm speechless. The sound was otherworldly, magical. John seems to arrive at an insight and declares in wonder, "God is truly mysterious." He looks at his mother, whose eyes are bright with tears, and reaches out his hand to her – she grabs it, shaking it in fierce agreement, and says, "Absolutely, boys, absolutely."

The next morning, I'm in the front yard with the family saying goodbye. They each stand almost formally, and again I'm startled by their respectfulness and courtesy. I can see the shadow of sadness in their eyes at my returning to the road – I don't want them to feel any more loss. It makes me even more reluctant to leave the warmth of these folks.

As if reading my thoughts, John says, "Why don't you stay a couple days, James? We'll cut some hay!"

We laugh, and I respond, "I got to get back on the road…something's out there."

"I understand," he says, totally getting it.

Kate wipes the perspiration from her face, tucking her work gloves in her back pocket; she has been out early, gardening in the gorgeous flower beds in front of the house. She steps forward, gives me a big hug, and whispers in my ear, "Not sure what you said to my son, but it brought him back, James. I knew in my heart you could. Thank you. God bless you. You're always welcome here."

"Thank you for making me feel at home," I reply. "It's meant a lot to me." Ever since I stepped foot on this special farm, my emotions have been very high and on the surface; I start to choke up, trying my best to push the feelings back down. It's her and her family that have helped me.

"Laura and April. Thank you for your hospitality – I really appreciate it." I hope they know I mean it.

"You're a fine musician, James," Laura says, and I can tell this is a young woman who does not hand out compliments often. But in this moment, her toughness seems to have softened. John told me she was her dad's right-hand around the farm.

April's sky-blue eyes haven't left me since we came out to say goodbye, and it's like she is waiting to tell me something. She reaches out to shake my hand, stepping close to me so no one else can hear. "In my short life, I have never heard anything like the one voice that came out of you and my brother. I will never forget it. Thank you, James. God's speed."

My heart fills with gratitude. I put my other hand over hers and try to get the words out through the overwhelming emotion surging up in me. "I won't either, April. Thank you."

I squat down in front of Joshua, "See this guitar pick?" I show it to him. "I've had it a long time; it's brought me luck, so it's very special to me. It's for you, pal."

"Wow! Really?" he exclaims, his farm-tanned face lighting up with surprise.

"Absolutely!"

"Thank you!" He catches me off guard and gives me a quick hug.

"I'll walk you to the car," John says. When we arrive at the driver's side, he stands tall in front of me with that proud-quiet-bearing like when I first saw him on the road. Looking at me with a purposeful intensity, he says, "Listen, just like my Dad told *me*, as far as I'm concerned, *the earth is in your voice* – you hear me, brother?"

As our eyes stay locked, a fierce sense of brotherhood flows up inside me, matching his. We communicate without words. This feeling of allegiance with another man feels familiar to me, empowering. He grabs me in a big bear hug and says, "Keep your eyes along the skyline, James. You never know what you can hear out there."

CHAPTER TWENTY-FOUR
Char Montgomery

I'm back in my office the next day, caught between trying to accept that it just might not happen with James and hoping the phone will ring and it will be him. All the promo shots of guitarists are scattered in a jumble across my desk. I'm resisting sweeping them on the floor in a fit of frustration.

The intercom buzzes: "Red to Char, Red to Char, come in." You have to laugh at this girl.

"Whose heart have you broken now?!" I say, trying not to laugh.

"It's not my fault!" she screams.

"What's up?"

"The big boss wants to see you."

"Great! I'm on my way."

I head out the door and hear Red's admonishment as I pass by, "Be cool."

I wink at her in response and head to the elevators and the upper floor. Eric sits behind his desk. When he sees me, he seems a little nervous.

"He's waiting. I'll tell him you're…"

I just ignore him, knock, and go in.

Jason Chandler sits behind his desk. At forty-nine years old, he doesn't look like the same man who started this record label when he was twenty-five, back in the day when music was really changing. Somewhere along the way, he took a detour from his original vision and sold out – a little. I've seen pictures of him back then: cool, relaxed, pony-tail; now he's always in $2,000 custom-made suits and $1,000 shoes, with a $100 haircut, fronting a stern-face. Every once in a while, he loosens up with me.

"You wanted to see me, Boss?"

"Stop calling me 'Boss'!" he admonishes me for the umpteenth time. His office is floor-to-ceiling windows, expensive contemporary furniture, and a giant glass-topped desk.

I try not to laugh. I sense he secretly likes it; everyone is intimidated by him.

"What's the status on your band?" he asks flatly, and suddenly the flicker of emotion from our ritual banter is gone.

"We're still auditioning front-men," I respond, matching his business-tone.

"I heard. What's the problem?" He challenges me, like what could possibly be the issue with finding a lead guitarist?

"No problem. I just haven't found him yet." I feel myself starting to heat up inside and try to hide it, taking a breath to release it.

"You're spending way too much time on this, Char," he says, giving me his friendly face that he hired me with.

I can sense he's losing confidence in me, so I go with what has always worked, which is to speak from my heart. "I want to get it right."

"Look, I'm swimming in demo-tapes from groups that already exist. They've already got some time together. You hear what I'm saying? I need you out in the clubs, on the road, looking at these groups, not auditioning every guitarist from here to London for a group that only exists in your head. You've gone way overboard on this."

"Only in my head!" I hear myself yell. So much for "cool"!

"Yes, that's right. Your time is what I'm paying for, and I want it used more responsibly. So, I want the project shelved." He announces this with that unbending facial expression I have seen before – meaning no discussion. I chuckle inside, saying to myself, *I guess he forgot…*

"Shelved! I got a year in this now. Isn't this why you hired me, to make these judgments? Do you remember what you said to me? 'Char, you got the ear. I need people like you working for me. Get some real music up in this brothel. You got an open checkbook.'"

"Brothel?" he asks, a confused look on his face.

"Sorry, your exact words were, 'house of prostitution.'"

He laughs and says, "I recollect something like that." He stands up, turning his back to me, and gazes out the big windows behind his desk at the skyscrapers of Manhattan.

Then, over his shoulder, he says, "You're quite a pistol, Char. Is that an expression they would use back in Big Sky Country?" Even though I can't see his face, I sense him smiling.

"Pretty close, Boss."

He turns to me. "Char, listen, I know you're looking for something – a sound, eh?" The guy who loves music peeks out in his tone. "We're all looking for that sound, that's why we're in this business. But sometimes what we hear up here…" he points to his head. "…isn't ready to come out. You know what I'm trying to say?"

"It *is* ready to come out. I can see it! It's right there in front of me. Give me another two weeks, and I'll show you."

We stare at each other. I hope every tough moment I have overcome from the day I was born is shining in my eyes. I feel him trying to look deep inside me, maybe looking at himself, because he seems to recognize me suddenly.

"Okay, two weeks. Then I pull the project. Understood? Don't let me down."

"Yes, sir."

I head back to my office and announce to Red with finality as I pass by her desk, "Two weeks." She nods, a glum look on her pretty face.

I close my door and survey my office, my eyes settling on the worn, black, rectangular guitar case – my talisman. "Okay," I say out loud, accepting the two-week deadline. "Figure this out, Charlotte." I recollect a saying I heard once, "When you come to the end of *the natural*, time to invite *the supernatural.*"

I go over to my old desk with its history of the West etched in each ornate section and unlock one of the top drawers. Inside is a small deerskin pouch. It contains my Wolf Medicine; it's sacred and contains all the moments of connection with my Wolf-Sister.

What is in the medicine pouch is a secret – don't ever tell anyone what's in your medicine bundle or your totem's name, my friends.

I lock the office door and sit cross-legged on the floor in the center of the room, holding my bundle against my heart, and close my eyes, quieting my energy for a minute.

"Come, my Sister, come," I call formally to her. Without hesitation, I sense my Wolf-Sister sitting across from me, and then she lifts her head to the sky and howls in greeting – a sound that reaches to an ancient place inside my Spirit, where I connect with all that is mysterious and where the impossible can become possible. I return her howl in my mind: my co-workers don't need to hear me howling! I stare into her eyes, breathing with my whole body in rhythm with her – this is the way we connect our souls.

"My Sister, I greet you, my heart is full," I say across to her. In my mind, she communicates the same greeting to me. I begin to sing very softly a Native American chant that was handed down to me as a way of honoring her. She howls again in response. I feel her happiness at seeing me, which always makes my heart soar. To be honored with her friendship is everything to me.

I glance over at my special guitar case, feeling its energy. I sense her intuiting my feeling, my desire and wish. She howls again to confirm this – over time, I have learned the subtle difference in howls and their meanings.

With passion in my voice at what's possible, I encourage her with all my heart, "Yes, my Sister! Go find James!"

CHAPTER TWENTY-FIVE
James Ryder

After spending time with John and his family, I start to feel down; I guess I've gotten in my head about losing both my parents and not really having a family. I've been driving twelve straight hours today, and I just don't feel like stopping. I check the dashboard clock: 1:00 a.m. A sign comes up on the right: *Memphis - 5 Miles*, and then another sign a half-mile later: *Graceland – Exit 23*. I think, *Wow, I forgot this is where Elvis's house is.*

I take the exit, getting excited at the prospect of seeing where Elvis lived. I follow the signs to the mansion, and suddenly I'm in front of the infamous Graceland Gates decorated with black musical notes – the white-columned big house is lit up in the distance. I make a U-turn and park across the street and gaze out at this special place. He was such a big part of my dad and me. I remember all the Elvis movies we watched together, the dancing and singing in the living room. Elvis's music brought happiness to my dad's Spirit, which in turn made me happy. He never loved another woman after my mom passed, which he told me was his choice. It's not that he lived in sadness, but it was only music that really brought him alive. I sense my eyes closing and don't fight it, resting my head back on the seat, thinking, *I'll just take a quick nap.*

My nightmare comes up on me fast; everything is moving more *rapidly and out of control* – the frantic nature of it scares me. I accelerate through Hendrix's song, "Are You Experienced?" with his pounding electric guitar sound and frenzied psychedelic images rushing at me; then I see me and Dad dancing the twist to "Jailhouse Rock;" then I witness a Native American woman standing by the side of the road. Then I'm in the front of the white shack in the woods with seven chairs, which transitions into me screaming at my father, "Nobody will mess with my music," then I'm quickly thrust into the hospital room, watching my dad fading, knowing his death will be the end of the world for me – that I will be alone. Then I see Char, imploring me, "Why are you giving up?" Suddenly, I'm running in a panic through the woods; I turn like always to see who's next to me. I finally see him! It's a young black man, in his early twenties, dressed in ill-fitting, ragged clothing. He dashes ahead of me, imploring me to run faster, waving at me to hurry; the terror on his face chilling me to the bone. I sense I'm holding something in my left hand, but I can't make it out when I look down. I hear dogs barking, then the gunshot, and my eyes snap open to someone shaking my shoulder. It's a burly state trooper, dressed in a blue uniform and trooper hat, standing outside my car door.

"You can't park here, son," he says, friendly, understanding.

I come fully awake quickly, saying apologetically, "Yes, sir. Sorry, guess I nodded off."

"You're not the first," he chuckles. "Get to a motel and get some rest."

"Okay."

"Welcome to Memphis, and give this beauty a wash!" he announces, a twinkle of humor in his eyes as he checks out my Corvette, which has a week's worth of dust on it.

"Yes, sir," I answer with conviction – the state trooper is obviously channeling my father!

CHAPTER TWENTY-SIX
James Ryder

After a rough night's sleep, I walk out of the motel room into the morning, not feeling in the best of moods. The nightmare really rattled me with this new development – for all these years, the dream has remained the same. The expression of terror on the young black man's face felt so real, not like some movie. I can actually *still* sense the feeling of fear in my body. And Char was in the dream, which brings the last moments in my apartment with her back into focus – I feel like crap for how I treated her. I hadn't voiced this idea to myself until this moment, but I guess part of me hoped the nightmares would stop once I left New York.

I drive over to the interstate on-ramps and see two signs: *55 South to Mississippi* and *40 West to Arkansas.* The rear-view mirror tells me there is no one behind me, so I stop the car and stare hard at the two ramps pointing in two different directions. Quickly, I conclude Mississippi just doesn't feel right, and I pull out, the tire spinning towards Arkansas, continuing west. A part of me, tucked away deep inside, shouts, *WHAT ARE YOU DOING!?* I ignore it like always and gun the engine, accelerating. I feel defeated, sick.

CHAPTER TWENTY-SEVEN
James Ryder

I'm in Oklahoma now, off the highway on a side road; I've hardly stopped other than for gas. This is the first time since leaving New York I feel directionless. A voice inside me is saying, *Just stop and breathe a little, brother*; I wave it away. The land has opened up, and all around me are green rolling hills. It feels familiar, easing the tension in me a bit.

Something standing on a hillock a hundred yards up ahead on the right catches my attention. I scoot my Ray-Ban sunglasses down on my nose to see a little clearer. "What? A wolf! That can't be!" I say out loud in surprise. I quickly pull over on the shoulder to get a better look. She stands still and seems to be studying me, then she points her nose to the sky and lets out a big howl. "Yup, that would be a wolf," I chuckle to myself as I observe the wider head, thick black fur, and the way she hangs her neck. I have no idea what particular states in the USA wolves inhabit, but I don't think they're in Oklahoma. I want to jump out and get closer, but I'm concerned my movement will spook her. She hasn't budged but just keeps watching me. I decide to give it a try and ease out of the driver's seat and walk very slowly around to the other side of the car and continue another twenty feet in her direction. If I wasn't so blown away, I might have some sense to not get so close. *Man, she is beautiful*, I think. Suddenly, I hear what sounds like music in the distance; it becomes louder with each moment, and I recognize it as Native American singing and drumming – the heavy pronounced beat of a powwow drum is accompanied by men chanting in unison, and for some strange reason, I feel like I could sing along with them, like I know the words. I'm not sure how, but I sense they are calling out to someone, honoring someone – over and over again. I search around quickly, trying to figure out where it could be emanating from. There is not a soul in sight in any direction. When I turn back around, the wolf is gone!

"Oh, no!" I say aloud, super-disappointed. I scan the area, but she is nowhere in sight. The music fades, and then a sudden warm wind blows over me, causing me to go very still inside. My eyes start to well up with that sad feeling I get when the spiritual whispers are trying to flow in – I sense something ominous is present.

I think, *What the hell?* and let out a big howl: "ARH-WOOOOOOO." I smile to myself – that felt kind of good. I extend my listening, hoping to hear a howl come back in response.

Then I hear it far in the distance: "ARH-WOOOOOOOOOOOOOOOOOOOOOOO!"

I shout into the wind, a longing in my voice: "I hear

you. I'm here now...I'm here...tell me what I need to know."

CHAPTER TWENTY-EIGHT
Char Montgomery

No matter what happens with James, I have to keep the band going. I hustle in late for another round of auditions and find only George and Cody are there.

"Hey, sorry I'm late. Where's Mark?" I ask them.

George says apprehensively, "Didn't you speak to him?"

"I got a message to call him. I figured I'd speak to him here."

They both look down at the ground.

"What's going on?" I ask, suspicious.

"He got an offer for another gig and decided to take it," Cody says, reluctantly.

I just shake my head. The boss's ultimatum, and now this. I plop down in a chair, shocked into silence.

After a moment, George offers softly, "Maybe he wasn't right for us anyway, Char." I appreciate him trying to take care of me and speaking the truth. I was fearful of letting go of Mark and how the company might react if I am two band members down.

I look up at them. "You're right, he wasn't a fit, was he?"

They both shake their heads reluctantly, agreeing with me.

I know I have to get some distance from everyone, so keeping my voice light (unlike how I'm really feeling), I say to them, "Look, let's call it a day. Tell these guys the auditions are cancelled for today. Red will call them to reschedule. I'll talk to you guys later." I peer directly in their eyes. "I don't want you both to sweat this. Okay?" They nod their heads at me, but I can see the concern in their eyes. This was a dream come true for them, and now... "I got a special friend working on this," I say to reassure them. "Just hang in there."

Something in my instinct says go visit Robert and his mom, Joan, which I have done a few times. I feel like they have adopted me! I grab the subway uptown and try not to hear the vestiges of James's guitar echoing off the walls, penetrating my soul.

Robert and I have special knock-code. It's the drum beat from a Hendrix song. I tap their door in the code, and I hear a yell from the back of the apartment, "It's Char!" and his mother responding, "Then go open the door!" I smile, happy I am so welcome – it really feels like back home and the neighborly way folks treat each other in the Northern Plains.

Joan and Robert won't let me decline their invitation to stay for dinner under any circumstances. I am deeply grateful for their hospitality. It's my third dinner with them, and each time, they help me forget the *hard world* outside their front door.

Joan shared with me that her ex, Robert's father, has been showing up less and less in the last six months. Initially, Robert was taking it pretty hard, but James's friendship made it easier for him. She said that even though James is gone on a road-trip, Robert seems okay. She thought he'd more upset, but he told her that James had been thinking about doing this for a long time, so it didn't surprise him.

Right now, Robert is in a deep debate with his mom over why he shouldn't eat his vegetables.

Joan comes in with the *killer close:* "Well, Char told me that when Jimmy Page was a kid, he ate lots of vegetables because it helped his fingering on the guitar."

Robert pretty much jumps out of his seat, "Jimmy Page of Led Zeppelin?!" he shouts.

Joan responds like it's not a big deal, keeping a straight face, "Sure, Jimmy from Zeppelin."

Robert shifts attention to me for confirmation, like this could not be possible. "Char, how do you know that about Jimmy?"

"He told me," I say, with the same no-big-deal attitude as Joan.

He literally flies out his chair and stands, vibrating as if he is going to take off into orbit. He practically yells, "You know Jimmy Page?"

"Sure, I met him a few times. Cool cat."

He stares at me, not really sure what to say next, kind

of stunned.

Joan and I just go about our business of enjoying the meal.

"Joan, can I have the rest of those green beans? They are really yummy."

"Sure." She hands the bowl to me, keeping a straight face.

Robert yells, "No wait!"

CHAPTER TWENTY-NINE
Char Montgomery

I'm back at the office the next day feeling a little a better. I recollect an old adage I like but only force myself to activate once in a while: *When in doubt, take a nap!* So, I decide to lie down on the leather couch and close my eyes for a few moments. I put Native American powwow music on the turntable.

Before I know it, I'm dozing off. Most of my dreams are about back home, especially my time in the mountains on horseback or with wolves – there is a wolf pack in a secret place I have visited for years. They will let me get within a hundred feet of them – they know me, but I never get in their space. In this dream, I see my black Wolf-Sister ahead of me, turning her head to look back at me. I get the feeling she wants me to follow her. Suddenly, we are in a place of rolling green hills that reminds me of the Plains out west. She's stopped and studies something to her left; I follow her gaze and see James! He's standing near a cool-looking black Corvette and watching my Wolf-Sister. He seems emotionally tired. The wind blows around him, then he yells into the open landscape, but I can't make out what he's saying. I call to my Wolf-Sister in my mind, *"Did you hear what he said, my Sister?"* She turns to me and telepathically speaks to me in my mind, *"He said, 'I hear you. I'm here now... I'm here...tell me what I need to know.'"* I wake myself up and sit up like a shot. I know instinctively what he is saying – he is ready!

CHAPTER THIRTY
James Ryder

The moment with the wolf and the Native singing was almost like it didn't happen, but the experience connected me with that unknown place inside me where the music comes from. I liked hearing that plea I made into the wind: "I'm here...tell me..." – it felt true, authentic. I sense an openness in me trying to form. I decide to pull over and get some lunch in a small, one-street town that has Americana written all over it. Life appears simple here: family-owned stores, a one-marquee movie theatre and, of course, an old-fashioned drive-up burger joint with waitresses on roller-skates! I stop and have something to eat and enjoy talking with a handful of high-school kids who come over to ogle the Corvette. My dad would have loved the way the car attracts people.

I finish up and drive onto the main street and stop at a red light. A fire-engine-red Dodge Charger R/T Hemi pulls up next to me and revs its engine twice. A girl in her early twenties sits behind the wheel – a real heartbreaker, thick, long brunette hair, with a cocky look in her eyes; you just know she's trouble! I chuckle, thinking, *Just too perfect!* She juts her chin forward, challenging me, then gives me the "smile" and revs her engine again. I hear Black Sabbath's "Iron Man" blasting out of her speakers. The song fits perfectly the aggressive stance of the Charger as its rear-end lifts up and down off her wide tires with each engine-rev – she rocks her head up and down, hair flying everywhere, to the drum beat, syncing herself inside the music.

Okay! I laugh inside and throw her my own "let's-see-what-you-got" smile and turn my head forward, narrowing my eyes and staring straight ahead, and revving the Corvette's big engine in response. Reaching down to the driver's side-door pocket, I retrieve an eight-track tape and, with a shift of one eye, check the label: WARNING: USE WITH EXTREME CAUTION. I slide the tape into the deck, turning the volume knob up. Elton John's "Bennie and the Jets" comes pounding out of the speakers. The movie, *Aloha, Bobby and Rose*, convinced me this was the perfect drag-race music. I gun the engine in staggered rhythm to the music. As a teenager, I imagined this moment a thousand times – with this music! I must be dreaming! The deep roar of the engines is bouncing off the store windows on either side. The street in front of us is suddenly deserted.

A final glance at my competition confirms her readiness – her eyes are focused like lasers on the pending light change, a big grin spread across her face

as she gives her brunette hair a final shake, settling herself. Our two cars wind up all their power, ready to be
let loose. The light turns green! I let go of the clutch
and stomp the accelerator and our cars burst forward
like rockets down the two-lane street. In the drive-in,
teenagers hanging out around their cars lift their heads
at the roar of our engines. We race side-by-side past the
kids who whoop and holler, cheering. I give the girl a
quick look, and she smiles like a devil at me and shifts
gears, shooting ahead.

"Too cool!" I shout inside the car. I shoot my fist in
the air out the window in salute. She returns my salute,
pumping her fist skyward. I feel better! Welcome to
America!

CHAPTER THIRTY-ONE
James Ryder

I drive the Corvette through the open plains, an endless view of terrain on all sides – a haze of heat on the secondary road in front of me. I've been trying to get off the interstate and travel on what best-selling author, William Least Heat Moon, calls the "blue highways." My mood has lifted, and I'm really enjoying being in the wide-open part of the country – things feel possible out here. Suddenly, a rush of steam erupts from the Corvette's hood. I pull over quickly, jump out, and carefully open the hood to billowing steam.

I peer down the empty road in both directions and laugh in disbelief – not a soul!

"Sorry, Dad!" I say to the cloudless-sky above me, "I bet you're rolling over in your grave right now! I just had to do it – did you see that Hemi Charger?"

I take out the road atlas to try and figure out where I am. A strong wind comes up and ruffles my hair. My hearing picks up the sound of a car engine in the distance; peering down the road, I spot in the swirling dust the shape of an oncoming vehicle. I lay the atlas down on the car seat, the wind flipping the pages.

An old beat-up truck comes into view, and I wave my arms to get the attention of whoever's driving, hoping they will stop. Thankfully, the truck slows and parks in front of the Corvette. A short, elderly Native American woman gets out – she has a dark reddish complexion, a thick, gray, braided pony-tail hanging down her back, and she's dressed simply in a long skirt to the ground and several silver beaded necklaces around her neck. What stands out is the deep sense of happiness shining off her – it's an energy that immediately washes over me.

I call out to her, "Thanks for stopping, ma'am."

She smiles at me with simple modesty and says with a heavy accent, "Your car, it is sick, eh?"

"Yes, it is...."

She interrupts gently, "Don't worry about it, I help." She scans the engine and asks, expanding her beautiful smile, "Needs water, yes?" She seems very familiar to me. I kind of space-out, wondering where I have seen her before and mutter, "Yes, ma'am."

"There's water in the back of my truck," she tells me, pointing towards it.

I just keep staring at her and suddenly I feel a little dizzy; I wonder if the heat is getting to me. I finally register her request and respond, "Yeah, sure, I will get it." I hustle to her truck, find a big water can in the truck-bed and bring it back, handing it to her, not sure why I don't do it myself. I feel like I'm in a fog. She takes a rag out of her pocket and reaches to unscrew the radiator cap, and I yell, "No wait!" concerned the steam will rush out and burn her. She doesn't seem to hear me and, surprisingly, not much steam releases when she takes off the cap. After she pours the water in, she steps back and grins at me, seeming to be happy and grateful she can help – to me, she feels both old and young at the same time.

"I think it will be okay now," she reassures me as if speaking about caring for a sick child

"Thanks, I really appreciate this. Can I give you some money or something?"

She walks over to the side of the Corvette, moving closer to me, and peers directly in my eyes. Her closeness feels supportive – and her Spirit seems to be saying, *you are not alone in the world, son.*

She waves her hand dismissively and replies, "No, no, it's my pleasure." She glances down at the road atlas on the driver's seat, which I notice is flipped to the state of Mississippi. She asks excitedly, "You are going to Mississippi?"

I say quickly, caught off guard, "No, no…well … I was thinking about it."

She nods her head, indicates she understands, and then her face just lights up with the same joyfulness I saw when I first met her. "Have a good journey, James," she says, and turns. As she walks back to her truck, I stand there frozen.

When I hear her engine start, I snap out of it and dash up to her window.

"Wait! How did you know my name?"

All I see in her eyes is pure love, and she says like she is wrapping me in a warm blanket of hope, "You will fare well, son." And with that, she drives away, the strong wind coming suddenly up. I stare blankly after the truck until it's out of sight. It's as if I'm in a dream; my eyes search around the open landscape, wondering what is going on. Then, in one moment, the obvious crashes over me: it was the Native American woman from my nightmares!

"Oh my God, it was her…" I exclaim, standing in the middle of the empty road in the center of nowhere. "… It was her…that's just not possible." Feeling like I need to sit down, I rest myself gently on the hood of the Corvette, trying to absorb what just happened. No matter what, I cannot deny it was her. I recall what she asked and retrieve the road atlas – a small piece of paper falls out. Curious what it is, I pick it up off the ground and read what's written:

"Dear Son, when you get to Mississippi, look up a man by the name of Pops – a good friend from way back. The town he lives in is circled on the map. He's on Tulip-Jasmine Lane. Good luck. I love you a lot, Dad."

I stare down at the note, confused, and say out loud, "How does he know someone in Mississippi? Who is Pops?" At the mention of Pops, I sense my heart race a little. I trace the route with my finger to the town.

The whispers are now *shouting* at me – it's time to listen.

CHAPTER THIRTY-TWO
Char Montgomery

I'm listening to Native American powwow music in my office – it makes me feel my Spirit. The intercom buzzes, and Red's voice says, "Char, there is a good-looking cat out here who says to tell you, the 'Backup' is here." I can hear the smile in her voice.

"Awesome!" I reply. I jump up and open my office door quickly to find Robert chatting with Red.

"Char," he says, "I don't understand, Maria told me she doesn't date musicians either. Maybe I should give up the guitar!"

"What! I thought you asked *me* out!" I counter, playfully affronted.

"I can't wait forever!" he shoots back, his eyes gleaming with mischievousness as always. "My mom told me to tell you, she'll be back in an hour. I told her not worry about me, and she said, 'No reason to worry, you're with Char Montgomery; I saw right away what kind of stock she's from.' What did that mean?"

Boy, I needed to hear that today. I thank the Creator in my mind for that kindness. "It means your mom is the kindest human being in the world! Come in and check out my office."

Robert walks through the door and right away asks me, "What's that music?"

"That's from where I live out in Montana. It's Native American powwow music."

"I like it a lot!" He moves his head up and down in rhythm with the pronounced heavy drum beat. He scans the office, fascinated with everything he sees.

"This is your office?" he asks, a little awed.

"This is the place!" His curiosity makes me feel like I'm a kid again, experiencing the world of music for the first time.

"Wow, cool. You have a lot of posters like James." He checks out the Led Zeppelin poster and points. "Char, is that the band's autograph?!" he asks, astonished.

"Yup! Pretty cool, huh?"

"Wow! You really do know Jimmy." He runs his little fingers over the four signatures.

The wolf photos catch his attention, especially the black wolf peeking between the trees. He glances at me and then back at the picture as if to check something.

Suddenly, startling me, Robert lets out a big howl, "ARH-WOOOOOOOOO."

Then I hear my Wolf-Sister let out a howl in response, "ARH-WOOOOO." I sense her sitting on her haunches next to me.

Robert turns around and stares at where my Sister sits

and says, "Cool!"

I'm confused. Then he says, pointing at the photograph, "Char, this black wolf looks just like your wolf friend."

The energy in the office seems to hush. I'm so stunned and caught off guard, I'm not sure what to say. I go over to my stereo system and turn down the music to orientate myself.

"You see a wolf hanging around me?" I ask, trying to keep the disbelief out of my voice. The only one who has been able to see her is my adopted Crow grandfather.

Then he says, like it's no big deal, "Yeah, sure, I saw her the first day when you came to meet James. She looks very happy and likes you a lot. She just howled at me. That's her way of saying hello!"

He goes back to studying the wolf and then notices the rectangular, black guitar case sitting underneath. I can't see his face, but he takes one step back quickly like something has surprised him so much he needs to move away from it. After a moment, he moves back towards the case and reaches out very slowly and tentatively touches the worn leather case with the tips of his fingers. I instinctively stay quiet and give him his space. He wheels around and faces me – I didn't think ten-year-old boys could look that serious. I don't understand how, but I know he intuits what's in the case. All I can think to do is nod my head to indicate, Yes, you're right. We stand there for a long moment, staring at each other, lost in a mutual sensation of *deeply-feeling-something* – a place I have lived in and embraced since his age. It's good to know I'm not alone.

CHAPTER THIRTY-THREE
James Ryder

I peer up ahead through the bug-splattered windshield to see the sun, a giant ball of orange rising behind a big green sign: *Mississippi.* I pull over onto the shoulder and check the map, confirming which exit I need to take. I'm a bundle of nerves and excitement.

Later that day, I stop at a white-washed Old General Store on a country road in the middle of nowhere. I'm lost! On the way here, the Old South started to show itself in white-columned mansions fronted by manicured lawns and then as I drove further from the highway, I saw broken-down houses with poorly clothed black children playing out in the dirt yards – it made me feel sad and seemed strangely familiar to me at the same time.

I'm standing on the porch of the store having a Coke; it's been a long time since I experienced drinking soda from a bottle! I notice a plaque on the building: 1918. I study the surrounding overgrowth of green vegetation and big, overhanging willow trees. Two elderly black men are sitting behind me playing checkers, and I sense them scoping me out – both of them are in their late seventies, with leathered skin and hard, tired eyes. It's so quiet here, I can hear the slide of the checkers across the board. I turn to them, hoping they might be able to help me.

With the utmost politeness, I greet them, "Afternoon."

They glance up at me and just nod and go back to their game.

"Fine day," I offer.

"Is that your car over there?" one of them asks me, in a gravelly voice, as if he is assessing the Corvette for some purpose. He pushes his reading glasses further down his nose as he eyeballs my car.

"Yes, sir."

"Use to be a boy 'round 'ere had a car like that," he says to his companion.

The second man, who wears a straw hat, chimes in. "Mm-hmm. Sure did. Drove into the swamp one night." He shakes his head. "Never did find it."

The first man says back, "Mm-hmm. He go out there every night, looking." His emphatic tone reveals he's impressed by the car owner's persistence.

"Every night." His friend says, nodding.

I sense they might be just fooling with me, but I go along with it.

"Would you gentlemen know how far I am from Old Country Road 46?"

"You about two, three miles from it," says the first

man.

"Wow, I didn't know I was that close," I say, surprised.

"What you looking for?" the second man asks, a light suspicion in his tone.

"A road called Tulip-Jasmine Lane."

"Tulip-Jasmine Lane?" he repeats, wanting to confirm what I've just said. Both men stop playing checkers and narrow their eyes at me as if I have said something important.

"That's right, sir." They study me for a long moment, *seeing something about me*, and then they glance at the car again. Then the first man who spoke to me moves his head up and down as if making a decision.

"Well, son," he says, "you just head down this road here till you hit 46, make a right, then Tulip is your second right. It's hard to see, so keep your eye out. Ain't no sign there."

"Thank you, sir. "

They nod and go back to playing checkers.

As I walk towards my car, one of the men calls after me, "You watch out for them swamps, ya hear?" I turn back, smiling and wave. They wave back, grinning as if sending me off on an adventure.

CHAPTER THIRTY-FOUR
James Ryder

I'm traveling on a dirt road bordered by a swap and crossed by sunlight filtering through the dense trees. I glance down for a second to check the gauges, then look up to find a ninety-degree curve looming in front of me. "Oh, shit!" I yell. I turn the wheel too quickly, and the back-end swerves, skidding around the turn, almost going into the swamp. "That was close!" I exclaim, laughing, remembering the men's advice.

The swamps and overflowing vegetation slowly give way to fields of wild grass and friendlier trees. Every quarter-mile or so, a hundred yards off the road, I see seemingly deserted, dilapidated white-planked shacks.

I finally hit an old weathered sign: *46.* I turn down the road keeping my eye out for Tulip-Jasmine, mouthing to myself their caution: "It's hard to see, so keep your eye out."

I go another quarter-mile and stop, sensing I might have missed it, and back up slowly and spot what looks to be an old dirt road. I see a weather-beaten old sign laying in the grass: *Tulip-Jasmine Lane.* The grass is so high it conceals the tire tracks. I swing onto it and drive at a crawl, being careful to keep the car within the tracks, the grass brushing up against the fenders – open fields and a beautiful variety of trees are on both sides of me. Suddenly, I hear a sound to the right of me and stop the car quickly and sit very still – it's music!

I turn off the engine and, with breath held, keep listening. I hear the faint sound of a slide-guitar and a man singing. All the energy in my body stops, going deeply quiet. I get out of the car, shutting the door gently, careful not to make any loud noise. I walk through the field, where the grass is up to my knees, towards the music – concentrating all my focus on the sound. I look ahead and see a tiny white sharecropper's house set alone against a block of trees. Someone sits on the front porch playing the guitar. Moving through the trees to within fifty feet of the house, I squat on my haunches behind a big tree. I peek around the trunk and see that on the porch, sitting in a chair, is a tall, heavy-set, elderly black man in his early seventies. He's playing one of those old Delta tunes I've lived inside of for years. I watch and listen in a way I have never listened to anything in my life. Every word he sings, every note he plays pierces me deep inside, at a place of pure emotion. My eyes fill with tears. When the old blues musicians come to New York to play the clubs, I'm always there in the front row, but the depth of this man's voice is something I have never experienced – I feel history, I feel transported to another time.

Suddenly, a voice cuts through the haze I'm in: "You there. Come on over here."

I jump as if coming out of a dream. I hesitate, not sure what to do. The old man calls out to me again, insistent, "Come on over here, boy. Nothing to be afraid of." He's right. I feel afraid – of what, I'm not sure.

Tentatively, I walk towards him, and when I get within talking-distance, I stutter. "I'm sorry, sir...I didn't mean to bother you...I just heard the music and wanted to listen. I'm sorry for bothering you." I finish by looking down at the ground because what I see in this man's face feels overwhelming. I quickly wipe a tear from under my eye, embarrassed to be so emotional.

I sense him studying me and then glancing behind me at the Corvette.

"Looks like you put on some miles there," he comments, his voice tough but friendly at the same time.

"Yes, sir, been driving around the country."

"That so? Guess you better have a seat, set a spell."

I say quickly, "Well, I'm..."

He interrupts me, a little fatherly edge to his voice, "Where you rushing to, boy?"

When he confronts me with this simple question, it dawns on me that's what I've been doing for a number of days.

"Go ahead and sit down," he suggests, like what am I waiting for, what's the big deal?

I take a seat across from him and right away stare at

the old acoustic guitar lying on the wood-planked porch by his side. It appears so alive to me, I want to pick it up and hear its secrets. I have no idea how he makes it sing like that. He notices where my eyes are laser-focused.

"You play, boy?" That firm voice again.

I peer into his eyes, and what I see there feels a thousand years old. It's humbling. To tell this man I play guitar, given the magic of what I heard coming from him, seems offensive.

"Some, sir." I stare down at the ground.

"Just some?" he asks, not believing me, eyeing my fingers and the callouses I've acquired playing guitar.

"Well, nothing like I heard you playing." I hesitate because I don't want to appear pushy but then ask, "Maybe you can help me. I'm looking for a man called Pops."

"You the government?"

"No, sir!"

"Ain't no sirs 'round 'ere, boy."

I nod my head, getting his meaning.

I see him appraising me again – it doesn't feel scary to me. I understand he would do this with any stranger.

He finally says, "I'm Pops, been answering to it some forty years now."

I reach out my hand to him. "I'm James, nice to meet you." When he sees my extended hand, he seems caught off guard and stares blankly at my hand. Then he gazes into my eyes, gauging something, and then he reaches out and shakes my hand. His big hand is heavily-calloused; I feel a hard life in it.

"What you doing 'round these parts 'cept listening to some old man sing?"

"I'm not real sure, I just…" I stop, looking around the surrounding area, which seems to pull at me. I want to go explore.

"Your last name Ryder, boy?"

"What? Yes, sir! How did you know that?" I ask shocked.

"Been expectin' you a long time now," he tells me, getting up, and picking up his guitar.

"Did you know my dad?" I ask excitedly.

"Fine man. Respected. Hear he's with the Lord now." He opens the screen door and says to me as he walks into the house, "There's a room at the top of the stairs on the right. You can sleep there. Might take yourself a rest, looks like you could use it. We'll be going out about nine or so as always." Then, in a softened voice, he adds, "Nice to meet you too, James." The screen door bangs behind him. I watch him through the screen, feeling every step he makes as he slowly walks up the stairs – like my Spirit is moving with his Spirit. I stand there frozen, not sure what to do or what is going on here. I study the area in front of the house, trying to orientate myself; I don't know why, but I sense I have been here before.

CHAPTER THIRTY-FIVE
James Ryder

Pops was right. I needed rest and fell asleep quickly. Next thing I know, I'm in the nightmare, but this time I'm running in the woods next to the young black man who I finally saw. Like before, he's really scared. I hear the dogs barking frantically close by. My friend implores me to run faster. I sense I'm holding something in my hand, so I glance down and discover it's a guitar. I notice my friend is also holding a guitar by the neck. Suddenly there's a gunshot, the whizzing sound passing my ear, and then quickly another shot, and I feel myself fall on the ground. I scream, waking myself up, and sit bolt upright in the bed. Right away, I see Pops, a concerned look on his face, his wide shoulders filling the space of the door.

"You alright, boy?" he asks. It feels comforting to hear the caring in the voice.

I stare long and hard at Pops's face – it's like he's trying to send a message to me. Even though I'm awake, the fear is still shooting through my nerve endings.

"Yeah, sorry, bad dream," I say, trying to shake it off.

"We all have 'um. Put some cold water on your face,

you'll feel better. About time to go. Grab that guitar I saw in your car."

"My guitar? How come? Where we going?" I ask, confused.

He looks across the room at me, the history of something unknown and deeply sad is in his eyes.

"You'll find out soon enough, James," he offers, an ominous tone in his voice.

CHAPTER THIRTY-SIX
James Ryder

Pops and I, both carrying our guitars, are walking along a moonlit dirt road bordered by densely packed trees on either side. The woods have a foreboding energy.

I ask him, feeling a little nervous, "Pops, where're we heading?"

"It's not much farther now," he tells me; I sense a heaviness in his answer. I don't know why, but I trust this man, and since my dad did, too, I don't offer any resistance to following him.

We walk on, surrounded by the sounds of the night, and five minutes later, Pops stops, checks the road ahead and behind us, then moves into the dark woods onto a thin trail. I follow behind; I can only see a few feet in front of me and keep my eyes pinned on Pops's back so I don't lose him. We walk deeper and deeper into the woods, then suddenly I hear the sound of music, and see a small light in the distance. As we step closer, the distinct sound of old Delta blues fills the air – it's haunting.

We come into a clearing, and every hair on my body stands straight up, and fear slams into me – in front of me are five black people playing instruments sitting on straight-backed wooden chairs in a quarter-circle in front of a decayed white shack – two chairs stand empty. It's the shack from my nightmare! I stop, frozen. Pops, sensing this, turns and motions with his head to follow him. His face is serious, dark with emotion. I don't know what else to do but trust Pops and trail him towards the musicians.

The group is comprised of a man in his early sixties, wearing an old suit jacket with a bow tie, playing slide guitar and singing; a rail-thin, tall man in his late forties, on a primitive stand-up bass; a man in his thirties and a teenage boy, both playing harmonicas – I sense they are father and son; and finally, a woman in a dark blue dress, in her late fifties, singing in accompaniment. Her demeanor reflects a steel-dignity that I sense has come from her getting beat up by life over and over again and never truly giving in.

No one looks or shifts their attention toward us, they just continue to play. Their eyes pained, absorbed in the music, stare straight ahead or at their individual instruments. Pops sits down in one of the empty chairs and indicates with his eyes for me to sit down next to him. *We're seven now*, I think, remembering the dream. Pops starts to play as if he has been sitting there all along; he just blends right into it. His face and eyes take on the same pained, lost quality as the others. I glance around, and I'm certain this is the place from my dream. It's so overwhelming, I don't know how to react. I'm stunned into a combination of emotions I have never experienced. I watch the others playing and sense there is something of great importance happening here, deep in the woods. I feel a familiar, dark seriousness come over my features as I listen to these people who continue to stare straight ahead into unknown lost places, as they play and sing with purity and simplicity from deep in their hearts, honoring their pain and their heritage. Pops starts to sing, his voice coming from some place inside where suffering lives.

Suddenly, as if a window opens in front of me, a vision appears before me:

I see a group of black people sitting on the porch of a shack playing music and singing and enjoying the evening. I don't know how, but I realize this is the past, and they are slaves. In the background, I see a plantation house. Suddenly, a white man runs up to them screaming, "Didn't I tell you niggers not to play that music?" He begins to whip them without mercy – the sight is horrifying in its brutality. Another image rushes into my vision: it's a juke joint bordering a swamp filled with music and people laughing – everyone seems so filled with joy and freedom. Suddenly, a dozen policemen raid it from all sides and attack the patrons viciously with large clubs as they flee in all directions – some are hit in the back of the head and drop to the ground – are they dead? Then I see a lone black man playing a slide guitar on the street of a small town. A sheriff and four deputies appear from nowhere and begin cursing him and drag him away, beating him repeatedly – the depth of hatred in their eyes is frightening. That scene blurs into another one of seven black people carrying instruments, traversing the woods, just as Pops and I did. They approach a lone shack surrounded by woods on all sides and scan the area suspiciously, fearfully. Suddenly the sounds of dogs and angry shouts can be heard in the distance. The people start to run frantically in all directions. In this vision, I follow two younger black men who spilt off from the group and sprint deeper into the woods. One man dashes in front of the other and turns, imploring his friend to run faster. Obviously, they're close buddies. The sound of men and dogs chasing them closes in. I notice the guitar in the young man's hand. Suddenly, there's a gunshot, and then another, and the young man's body flies forward, shot in the back...

I feel something hit my back from behind, my body lurches forward, and I grab my chest – it jolts me out of the vision, and I quickly sense Pops and the group sitting next to me. I feel panicked, out of breath. Then it all slams into me, and I press my palms against my face, trying to hold onto something.

"Oh, my God, oh, my God!" I cry. Tears fall down my face. "I understand, I understand."

I look over at my companions who continue to play. I whisper again, "I understand."

In the deepest respect, I purposely take my hand off my guitar and sit perfectly still, my back straight, my chin raised and watch these brave people – my heart full of a fierce reverence and pride.

CHAPTER THIRTY-SEVEN
James Ryder

The next day, I wake up early and sit on the front porch watching the newness of the morning as butterflies flutter through the tall grass and birds fly in and out singing. You can really smell the earth here in Mississippi – it makes me feel part of it. Pops comes out of the house, stretches his long arms to wake himself, and sits in the rocking chair. I notice the large size of his hands and forearms and know what it must have taken to form them. I sense he's done this same morning ritual for more years than I can count.

"Morning, Pops," I greet him.

"Morning. How'd you sleep, boy?" I appreciate Pops's fatherly manner; I'm really needing it after last night.

"Not real well." I feel exhausted emotionally. So much to take in from the journey in the woods.

"What's on your mind?" The gruffness, which is just natural to Pops, comes through in his voice; I'm starting to get that his toughness is really love in disguise.

I feel reluctant to speak. So many questions and no

questions at the same time – so much was answered last night.

"Mm-hmm. I see what's needed here!" Pops reaches for his guitar and starts to play an upbeat Delta tune and motions me to join in with a wave of his guitar.

I feel scared – I think because it means opening even more fully to who I really am – to embrace the deeper history in me. I shake my head, not having the words. Pops says, "You got it in you, James." Then, he hands me a piece of metal pipe to use as a slide.

I reach for my guitar and take the slide from Pops, which feels familiar in my hand. Over the years I have tried to feel comfortable with using a slide but kept moving away from it – I understand why now.

I watch Pops's hands closely and tentatively start to play, adapting to the slide.

An encouraging smile from Pops builds my confidence, and the sound of my guitar grows stronger. Pops starts to sing Robert Johnson's "Come On in My Kitchen," which I know from listening to his album countless times. Pops gestures with his hand to join his singing. I close my eyes, taking myself back to the shack last night and the sense of something ancient I felt. A connection is trying to flow up from deep inside me, and instead of being afraid of it, I open the door and let my voice come out of my soul, joining Pops in the lyrics. Our voices fill the porch, and suddenly I just feel deeply at home in myself, a feeling I hope with all my heart to experience more.

"All right! What did I tell you, boy?" Pops shouts, with a big grin spread across his wise face.

CHAPTER THIRTY-EIGHT
James Ryder

Pops and I sit quietly on the front porch watching the sun go down; a gentle breeze stirs the trees. I like being quiet with Pops. I just feel present here, with no thoughts running around inside my head. I have a few questions that I sense are okay to ask – meaning the desire to *ask* is not coming from frustration or need, but a different place.

I try and ease into it, given Pops's penchant for giving me a hard time! "Pops, can I ask you a strange question?"

"I don't see why not? You a strange sorta fellow, James," he answers back, chuckling, rocking back and forth in the chair.

"Thanks a lot!"

"Who says it's a strange question?" He asks in that hard-caring voice.

"Okay…Can I ask you or not?" I am learning to get a little cankerous with him myself. He seems to appreciate the pushback!

"I'm waiting." Pops tries to hide a grin, but I caught it!

"Okay, here it is: inside is this *feeling*...and I...never mind...it's nothing." I just shut down, frustrated at not having the words.

He stops rocking and says firmly, "What you trying to ask, boy? Must be something. You come a long way to find out." Like usual, he nails me again. We stare at each other until I know I have to make an effort out of respect for him.

"You see, inside is this feeling. It's like the feeling of sadness, and it makes me feel connected..." I just shake my head again, disappointed that I'm not able to explain this with clarity.

"Whose sadness you talking about?" he says, pushing me.

I think a moment and reflect back to my conversation with Char.

"Other people, it's other people's sadness," I answer quickly, a light bulb going off.

"And what are you seeing about those folks when their bad times are looking at you?"

I ask myself quietly, trying to prod the answer, "What am I seeing?" Then it dawns on me and I say, "I'm seeing their struggle...yeah, that's it...I see their dignity."

"What are you going to do about it, son?" he asks in an almost confrontational tone.

The question angers me for some reason, and I snap back at him, "What am I going to do about it?"

"You heard what I said. You a caring sort of person,

James. Stop hiding it." Then he peers deeply in my eyes and says what I have been waiting twenty years to hear: "Don't have to hide anymore. You hear what I'm saying, brother?"

I nod, finally understanding, my eyes filling. I repeat the words to myself just so I can truly hear them, "Don't have to hide anymore."

He adds, "Playing is like looking for something to give away. It's like trying to find a gift for folks." He goes back to rocking his chair and gazing out at the beautiful evening.

After a long silence, he pipes up, "Now, have at them dishes. What you think I'm running, one of them bed breakfast places here? Enough of this yapping!"

CHAPTER THIRTY-NINE
James Ryder

Two days later I walk out of the front of Pops's house, carrying my guitar and shoulder bag. I feel him coming behind me to join me on the porch.

"Good-looking morning," he announces brightly, observing the area.

I feel overwhelmed at the thought of leaving, but I know it's time.

"Where you heading?" he asks me, the father-vibe in his tone again.

"Up to Seattle. There's a friend there I have to visit."

Pops turns and looks at me, a little glint in his eyes, understanding. He knows who is up in Seattle. "You give him my best – fine musician."

"Okay." I can hardly get the words out, feeling a tidal wave of emotion trying to burst through. "I'll be back."

"Know you will. I will be here. Don't be rushing, now. A lot of country to see between here and there."

"Yes, sir."

"Ain't no sirs 'round here, boy, how many times do I have to tell you?"

I nod my head with conviction to let him know I get what he's telling me.

I shuffle my feet around, not wanting to say goodbye. It's hard to look at Pops: I'm fearful I will start to cry. Finally, I lift my head and find him smiling at me with a face full of pride. I am so grateful to this man. Unable to bear it any longer, I reach over and give the old man a big hug and whisper, "Thanks for everything."

Feeling the tears on my cheeks, I quickly pick up my things and walk towards the car, getting about twenty feet when Pops calls after me, "James…" I stop and look back at Pops standing on the porch, one hand leaning on the roof struts. "Lot of folks left us too early to keep the playing going, you hear?" His big voice cuts across the Delta high-grass, the courage of generations of struggle behind each one of his words.

The weight of that message pierces my soul so deeply, I'm afraid to speak. I can only shake my head up and down adamantly, the tears streaming down my face. Then he adds with an unbreakable voice, "Never forget where you came from, son."

I can't believe it! It's the same phrase my Dad left me. I say with all my heart, "I won't forget, Pops, I promise. You can count on me."

"Never doubted it, James. You got your father's manner about you."

CHAPTER FORTY

Char Montgomery

I'm walking down the hallway toward Red and my office after a long session auditioning drummers. Some good possibilities in what we saw, so I'm feeling more optimistic. As I near Red, I can immediately see she is not looking too happy.

"What's going on?" I ask her, concerned.

"The boss called."

"He wants to see me?"

"No, he just left a message." She hands it to me. I look down and read it:

From Mr. Chandler: *One more week. No exceptions.*

"Oh shit! Has it been a week already?" I ask.

Red nods, glum. In frustration, I crumple the paper in my hand and throw it into her wastepaper basket. Red and I stare at each, not really sure what to say.

"Red, I'm not to be disturbed for a while. Okay?"

"You got it," she responds, continuing to watch my face closely to see how I'm reacting.

I go into my office and shut the door behind me, locking it. I take a long moment, standing there, breathing, trying to let the sudden pressure out. I notice my talisman, the worn, black guitar case across the room, which Robert was drawn to. I'm still pretty blown away about how he discerned what was inside it and that he was also able to see my Wolf-Sister. I get an instinct to connect with my talisman, so I sit down, cross-legged, next to the case and lay it flat across my lap so my hands are resting on top of it. I close my eyes, letting what's inside the case flow deeply into my soul. I feel a presence in front of me and open my eyes to find my Wolf-Sister sitting, gazing at me. "A Ho, my Sister," I greet her. "A Ho," is a Native American term that can mean many things depending on the moment, but right now it means, "I am honored to see you."

She lets out a big howl in greeting, "ARH-WOOOOO."

I go totally silent inside, not *trying* to hear what she wants to communicate. I call it a *sacred-waiting*. Suddenly, I hear her voice speak one word inside me, "Robert."

I ask, "Robert can help me?" She lets out another howl in agreement. In my upbringing, you get a message, you follow it without question. "Okay, let's go see him and Joan." I lay the guitar case gently against the wall, jump up, grab my bag, and my Wolf-Sister and I head out the door.

"Red, I'll be back," I say, rushing to the elevator. I feel some hope. Spirit never lets me down.

———•◆•———

At their apartment, Robert lets me in after my Hen-drix-knock-code and, as usual, Joan spots my mood too well.

"Sit down, honey. You look worried."

"I guess I'm running out of time." I take a moment and then ask, "Robert, do you have any idea where James might have gone?"

Robert thinks a moment, then says, "He left me Jimi's album to watch for him, maybe he went to see Jimi."

"What do you mean?"

"You know, where Jimi is," he says, happy to talk about Hendrix.

"You mean where his grave is?"

"Yeah, outside of Seattle, Washington." He tells me this with such authority it feels like he's been there.

I think a long moment. Robert watches my wheels turn.

"Can I come?" he asks, excitedly.

"Where?"

"With you to Seattle!"

"You think I should go, huh?"

"Yup, as long as I can go. I don't take up much room."

Joan interjects, trying to be reasonable, "Robert, Char has important business, and you have school."

"Mom, the room is moving around, I feel kind of

hot." He mimes appearing dizzy and burning up.

"No!" Joan, says firmly, trying not to laugh.

"When are you going?" Robert presses me. This kid has got some cowboy in him.

I run through my schedule in my head and then think, *It doesn't matter.* "I guess I could fly out the day after tomorrow."

"Mom, could we go to the airport with Char? I love planes!"

"You'd have to ask her, sweetheart."

"Definitely!" I reply. "I hate going to airports by myself. It gets kind of lonely."

"That's the thing I'm best at!" he says.

"What?" I ask, not sure what he means.

"Helping Char not to be lonely!"

What do you say to that, folks?

CHAPTER FORTY-ONE
James Ryder

I've made it up to Chicago. It just felt right to stop here, given this was the path a lot of Delta musicians took coming out of the fields down south. I walk out of a 7-Eleven just off the interstate in a run-down section of the city and notice a half-dozen black people, some of them carrying instrument cases, walking down an alley. They seem out place on the deserted street. The voice inside me says, *Follow them.* I'm listening to the voice now with no hesitation and head to the alley entrance and peer down, spotting a small sign at the end: *Memphis Club.* I make the short walk to the entrance, and when I open the door, I'm met by the loud applause and yells of a good-sized crowd. The small, smoky nightclub is packed with mostly black patrons with a few whites here and there. The applause dies down, and I spot the stage where a combo of musicians is set up. The band goes into its next number – an upbeat blues song reminiscent of "Muddy Waters." I look around, and when I see how the crowd is really into the music, it makes me feel happy – that's a new feeling for me. When I used to go to clubs, seeing the performers jam would ignite feelings of self-judgment and disappointment in what I hadn't done. I couldn't stay away, even though going would make me feel stuck in the middle. Now, I'm free of all those negative thoughts. It's so cool to experience the power of music this way without a dark cloud around me.

The next day, I'm having lunch at a family restaurant just off the interstate, writing feverishly in my notebook; songs are just pouring out of me. The sadness is there but in a very different way. It doesn't feel oppressive, maybe because I know now where it comes from. I just feel grateful to be able to see folks deeply and to be in touch with what troubles them. I glance around the restaurant and notice a father and mother and four kids walk through the front door. The kids are all under eight and well-behaved. I notice the weariness around the parents' eyes; you can just sense they have seen some rough times. I check the parking lot and spot an old worn-out station wagon pulling a U-Haul; I'm sure it's theirs. I watch closely every step the family takes as they progress to their table led by the hostess. The father and mother carry themselves with a quiet dignity, and then at the table, the mother makes sure the kids are comfortable, fussing over them in a loving way. She gives each one of them a menu, which I can see is a big treat to them. I watch the parents exchange a quick glance at each other, and I can feel their obvious devotion to one another. The father nods at his wife, and what I hear in his mind is, *Don't worry, my love, we will make it back one day.* The obvious courage of these folks is inspiring. I seem to be seeing people more deeply since my stay with Pops – maybe I'm letting myself feel in ways I never had before.

CHAPTER FORTY-TWO

James Ryder

I follow Pops's advice and take my time on the way to Seattle. I'm anxious to see my "brother," Jimi Hendrix, but I know in my heart the old man was right – *slow down*. I think many guitarists consider Hendrix their brother. From what I can tell of film and books on him, he was a kind soul and very shy.

On the trip, I get led to some amazing places by just following that voice inside me: turn here, go straight. One day, I'm guided to an old ghost town in Wyoming – it's like something you'd see in a movie, but there is no one there. I sense the place at a deeper level, feeling its history, the same way I did with the family at the restaurant. My "seeing" the world has opened more fully, and it's exciting.

CHAPTER FORTY-THREE
Char Montgomery

Two days later, Robert and Joan are seeing me off at the airport gate at Kennedy. Robert has brought his guitar along so it could say goodbye to me too. The kid definitely speaks my language – everything is alive.

"Char, you won't forget to say hello to Jimi for me, right?" Robert reminds me.

"I won't forget. I promise," I say very seriously, so he knows I understand how important this is to him.

"And you'll tell James I've been practicing, right?"

"I'll tell him...if I find him, okay?"

"Oh yeah, of course, sure."

Then I tell him, kind of distractedly, "Listen, you know what? No, never mind, you probably want to go to school or something, never mind."

"What? What about school? What are you talking about?" he asks, confused.

"Well, I don't know if I told you, but I get a little scared on planes by myself, and I was thinking...well... what would you think about coming along, helping me find James, and visiting Jimi?"

"What! Really?!" His eyes bug out of his head.

Robert turns quickly to his mother, who holds his ticket out to him.

"Here's your ticket, honey!" Joan says, her face full of such joy to give her son the ultimate wish. The fact that she suggested this to me and is willing to let me take her ten-year-old boy on a trip across the country blows me away. I offered to take her too, but she said no, she felt in her heart that her son needed to do this alone with me to watch over him. "You're a special woman, Char," Joan had said. "I know my boy is in good hands."

"Mom, you're kidding me, right?!"

Joan gives him a long hug and says, "You go with Char, and help her find James."

CHAPTER FORTY-FOUR
James Ryder

I'm driving on one of those blue highways and notice up ahead through a bug-splattered windshield a drab, isolated, large one-story building set against a background of twilight sky and snow-capped mountains. A marquee borders the road: *The Last Ditch Saloon, Bar/Restaurant, Live Music.*

I really need to use the restroom. The Corvette rumbles across the dirt parking lot, and I park in front of the entrance; there is just one old pick-up in the lot. I get out stiffly and stretch, feeling the coldness of the clean air hit my skin. As I near the entrance of the bar, I hear the massive sound of a complex drum solo – whoever it is has some real talent. I stop short, suddenly identifying the song, and say out loud, "Wow, that's Ron Bushy's drumsolo from 'In-A-Gadda-Da-Vida'! Iron Butterfly!"

Just like when I was a kid, I close my eyes so I can really absorb the drumming. My body and head start to rock to its rhythm. The sound pulses through every part of me until all I can feel is the drums deep inside me, consuming me. My hands start to play air drums in sync, my wrists flicking and hitting each lick – I'm totally lost in the sound. A car driving by blasts its horn, and I'm suddenly snapped out it. *Wow!* I think, *I was really gone there for a second.* I can't wait to meet this drummer, so I open the big front door, and the drumming immediately stops. The inside of the bar is large and dimly lit with a long, flat bar on the right and dozens of tiny round tables and vinyl-backed chairs. I hear a man's semi-perturbed voice from the back of the room, "Place is closed!"

"What time do you open up?" I call across the bar, wondering if the voice is the drummer. I squint my eyes trying to see him.

"Seven," he tells me, seeming none too happy with my intrusion.

"Okay. All right if I use the rest room?"

I hear an exasperated sigh from him.

"I'll just be a minute," I offer.

A long moment, and then he says, resigned, "It's over here by the bandstand."

"Thanks." I wind my way through the tables, which seem to go on and on, and I discover the man attached to the voice is sitting behind a professional Ludwig drum kit with oversized drums. He's holding drumsticks and is a hardened man, very serious eyes, not someone you want to fool with. He's average height, in his early forties, but with youthful, longish hair tucked behind his ears, a blue denim work-shirt with the sleeves rolled up, and a slight bead of perspiration on his forehead. Even though he's no longer touching the drums, what strikes me is the energy that still seems to be vibrating between him and the drum kit; I've never felt anything like it. He appears physically connected to the instrument – it's tangible. The power of it stops me short at the edge of the stage, and we study each other for a long moment. Unconsciously, I nod my head firmly in acknowledgment of what I have just witnessed and felt – that I understand I got in the way of his practice session.

He points with a drumstick, "It's over there." His voice seems to have softened.

"Thanks." I start to walk over, moving closer to him. "I really like that rhythm you were playing. Pretty heavy."

"Really?" He seems shocked I would notice, which surprises me because I think someone with that kind of talent would receive a lot of compliments.

"Reminded me of John Bonham's style." He was Led Zeppelin's drummer.

His eyes widen. "Don't know about that, but I appreciate it, partner."

"Can you tell me where the hell I am?" I say jovially, sensing the ice is broken.

"Son, this is Big Sky Country," he chuckles.

"It surely is," I smile, glad the tension has eased.

"Where you from?" he asks me.

"New York."

"Long way," he says knowingly, understanding the journey as if he's been there.

I nod, feeling the weight of the trip.

"I'm James," I say, reaching out my hand across the drums.

"Sam." He leans forward and shakes my hand. "Nice to meet you."

"Likewise."

"Visiting folks around here?" he asks.

"No, just traveling around."

"Been a long time since I did that. Some good old times." He seems to reflect on his own memories, then asks, "What kind of wheels you driving?" I laugh inside; Sam is just like my dad, getting right to what's important.

"'67 'Vette."

"Don't know why but had a sense you were driving a rocket. 427?"

"You got it," I say smiling.

"They don't make them like they used to."

"I hear you." I sense Sam is like me and enjoys the pleasure of talking with someone; the road can get lonely.

I scan around the expansive bar, checking it out, "What kind of music do you play in here?"

Sam seems to hesitate, then says quickly, "Country, rock, whatever it is, it gets these cowboys to beat up on each other pretty quick."

"That was the drum solo from 'In-A-Gadda-Da-Vida' you were playing?"

Sam looks over at me surprised and a little taken aback, "You recognized it?"

"Absolutely, you were inside the pocket."

Sam seems uncomfortable hearing my compliment. "Do you play?" he asks me. There is a sudden hopefulness in his voice.

"Guitar." This simple word feels different coming out of me; like I'm partnered to the guitar at an even deeper place.

Sam thinks a moment, then says, "You don't have it with you, do you?"

"Yeah, sure."

"Do you want to jam a little?" he asks, that hopeful vibe in his voice again.

"Right now?" I respond, surprised. I actually feel myself back up a step.

"Sure, we got a couple hours before they open up."

Suddenly, I feel super-apprehensive – this will be the first time I'm playing with a professional musician. Sam watches me intently, waiting for an answer.

"Hey, man, you play every chance you can get, right?" I can sense the intensity and wanting in his voice. Not sure why it's that important to him; I'm sure he plays all the time with that kind of talent.

I stare at the bandstand, the drum set, and time seems

to stand still. I can feel my heart beating. I know there is only one decision to make.

"Okay, brother. I will go get it."

CHAPTER FORTY-FIVE

James Ryder

I retrieve my guitar and walk again through the winding path of tables and chairs. I feel a nervousness in my stomach and try to breathe to release it. I see Sam sitting silently, waiting for me. I locate an amp, switch it on, plug in, and make sure my Stratocaster is in tune. These ritualistic actions calm my Spirit. I feel a focused silence flow into me. The notes from the tuning sound enormous in the bar.

"What should we play?" I ask him.

"Cream's 'White Room'?" he asks hesitantly, almost a little shyly like he's not sure I will know it.

"Cool." I respond – my kind of music. I get behind the mic stand and turn it on. "Test, test." I turn to Sam and nod, and he counts us in with drumsticks, "Ah one, two…"

I open up with Clapton's great guitar riffs, which I have practiced countless times, and Sam comes right in mirroring Ginger Baker's strong drum sound. I take a quick glance at Sam, and I'm a little shocked at how his physical presence has transformed – it's pure concentration and fierce power. You wouldn't know he's the same person. We play in immediate synchronization and exchange admiring smiles. I lose myself in the experience of having my guitar sound supported by the power of a full set of drums for the first time. My whole body is rushing with feeling. I felt this with Lucas, my pail-drum partner back on the street in New York, but never to this depth and intensity. I turn my body sideways every once in a while so I can stay connected to Sam. He attacks the drums with a controlled ferocity, which truly reminds me of John Bonham. Every one of his drum hits feels connected to my guitar – there is no space between where he starts and where I pick up – a sacred merging. An intense gratitude and joy spread through me – it's intoxicating. We finish the song, leaving the big room filled with an awkward silence. I'm nervous about turning around and looking at Sam, fearing some judgment. But I quickly realize it would be rude not to acknowledge him.

When I finally make eye contact with Sam, I see he's staring hard at me, his brow knitted like there is something he doesn't understand.

"And you're just traveling through?" he asks, bafflement in his tone.

I nod, not able to speak.

"And you just pulled over here to use the restroom?"

"Yeah," I say softly, understanding the underlying message in his questions.

"Where do I find your albums?" he asks, grinning like it's time for me to stop pulling his leg.

"It's just me, Sam." I hear myself speak the words, and the exposed heaviness of them makes me feel the hard truth about my life – I've been alone for too long.

Sam nods, the expression on his tough face telling me he can relate, which in turn makes me feel like there wasn't something *wrong* with me all these years.

He says, "Thanks for doing this." I'm not sure why, but jamming together seems to mean as much for him as it does for me.

"Sure." I hesitate a moment, then take a leap. "I've got something I've been working on. Can we give it a try?"

"Let's do it!" Sam responds, excited.

I start to play one of the songs I have been working on for years. It comes from the *whispers – but now they are no longer whispers but shouts that I will not ignore.*

CHAPTER FORTY-SIX
James Ryder

Sam and I sit at the long bar after jamming to one of my songs.

"You really got something there, James. Thanks for letting me work on it with you." Even though I have only known Sam an hour, it takes me only a minute to get he doesn't waste words or is someone who offers a compliment just to be nice.

"No, thank you. Honored to play with you. What time you open up? Maybe I will hang around, hear you play."

In a heartbeat, Sam becomes super-nervous, and there's a hesitation in his voice as he says, "Um...we don't...it's our night off."

"Friday night?" I question.

"Well...um...see, there is some sort of problem with electricity." He points, indicating the darkness of the room. "In fact, I better be closing up before you can't see anything in here."

I'm confused, but it seems impolite to question him. I am so grateful to have met him and to have had this experience.

"Okay, sure. Hey, I really enjoyed this. Thanks."

Sam says heavily, "Me too."

We stand there awkwardly, not knowing how to part, and finally, Sam extends his hand.

"Take care." Sam offers, looking into my face like he is trying to remember it.

"You too, thanks again."

I walk out to the parking lot, and as I'm about to open the car door, I stop, shaking my head in disbelief and say out loud, "Damn, I forgot to use the bathroom."

I go back, open the front entrance door, and hear the juke box playing some Steppenwolf really loud, completely filling the bar space. I step inside the darkened room and stop short – on the other side of the room, Sam, whose back is to me, is hunched over mopping the floor, a bucket and cart of cleaning utensils by his side. In an instant, I understand what his nervousness was about. Every part of me inside goes quiet, absorbing the truth of what just happened; a fierce allegiance strains my eyes. As slowly and quietly as I can, I back up, open the door behind me, and then raise my fist in front of my chest to Sam and whisper, "You play every chance you get, brother." I bow my head in respect.

CHAPTER FORTY-SEVEN
Char Montgomery

Robert and I are settled into first class on the plane. He keeps looking down the aisle where the flight attendant has stored his guitar.

"Char, I don't think my guitar is very happy over there in that closet."

"I know, pal, but they have to keep it there so nothing happens to it. Don't worry, I'm watching it. And you know how I feel about guitars."

"Okay." He scans the cabin, checking things out. "Char, this is first class, right?"

"Yup, on the record company."

"So, when I become a rock & roll legend, this will be my seat when I'm on tour?"

"No, at that point, you will have your own plane. Cool, huh?"

"Wow!" He thinks a moment, then says, "Don't worry, you can still sit next to me, I won't get a big head."

At that exact moment, the flight attendant who stored his guitar approaches us, and Robert says, "Sorry, no autographs, Miss."

The flight attendant goes along with it. "I understand. Perhaps when you are deplaning?"

He points at me and says, "You'll have to ask my representation."

An hour later, after a good nap for the both of us, I glance over at my pal and see he's having the time of his life, checking out the headphones and different music stations. I want to ask him a question but feel a little nervous. When he takes a listening break and goes to reach for the airline magazines, I say, "Do you think James will like it if we find him? You know what I mean? Do you think, he'll feel I'm really..."

He finishes my sentence for me, "...being too pushy?" I see him trying to suppress a smile.

"You were listening?"

"When?" He feigns total innocence of my conversation through James's door.

"Okay. What do you think, Backup?"

He leans over and whispers to me like it's secret: "Rock & Roll."

"Rock & Roll?" I ask confused, keeping my voice low too.

He smiles at me and mimes fingering his guitar, his face lost in the music.

I get it. "Okay, Backup." The *search is my music*, so stop thinking and just rock out!

Robert opens a travel magazine, flipping slowly through the pages; I notice before each turn of the page, he tilts the pages to the right.

"Kiddo, I'm curious about something. Why do you keep tilting the magazine before you turn the page?"

"Your Wolf-Sister is looking at the pictures with me. We like checking out the different places you can go." He hesitates a moment, then adds, "It's good she is along with us – I bet wolves are awesome at finding people."

"She is, Backup, she is," I confirm, smiling at the truth of that. I think gratefully, *You wouldn't be sitting here helping me if it wasn't for her – making me feel not so alone. I say, A Ho to my Wolf-Sister.* When one's feelings or gratitude are so deep that there are no possible words to express them, that is also "A Ho."

———•·•———

Before I know it, we are landing in Seattle, and I'm trying not to tell myself for the umpteenth time that this search for James is absolutely crazy. But then in the next moment, I keep going back to when folks would ask me why I ride wild broncs, telling me I could be easily killed or really injured – even paralyzed – I only had one answer: I'd jab two fingers against my heart twice, meaning it's what my heart wants, that's all that matters – period.

We arrive at the shiny metal baggage turnstile, which Robert keeps examining. "What's this?" he inquires.

"It's what our baggage comes in on. It's like a big conveyor belt. So, what do you want to see in Seattle?" I ask him, more to ease my nervousness about our crazy quest. I wonder about the true source of my anxiety – searching for James or completing my dream band.

"James won't be here till tomorrow," Robert says simply, announcing this fact as if it's no big deal.

"What? How do you know that?" I ask him, confused.

The turnstile starts to operate. "Char, look! Cool!" he yells and jumps on, then quickly jumps off. "It's going really fast! Our stuff won't go back to New York, will it?"

"No, it will be all right. What do you mean James won't be here until tomorrow?"

Robert turns and gazes at me with those *knowing eyes* I have come to know as I've spent more time with him. The sounds around us quiet. He doesn't take his eyes from mine – the dark seriousness present again.

I nod my head, "Okay. Tomorrow, kiddo."

CHAPTER FORTY-EIGHT
James Ryder,

The night sky is filled with stars; I shift into fourth gear as I get back on the highway after having dinner at a cozy family restaurant just off the interstate. I have found so many wonderful family-run restaurants on my trip. The friendliness of folks keeps filling me with kindness. A sign comes up: *Seattle, Washington 90 miles.*

I say out loud in the car, "I'm almost there, brother," and then punch a new eight-track into the stereo – "Purple Haze" comes blasting out of the speakers.

Early the next morning, I pull up to the cemetery entrance and look at the iron-gated archway: *Greenwood Memorial Park – North Entrance. Wow*, I muse, *it took a long time to get to this place.* I feel nervous, excited, grateful. I drive through the well-groomed landscaping and peer out at the small, numbered green signs that border the road indicating the section numbers. I spot the number I am searching for, pull over, and take a moment to gaze over the headstones, looking for where I believe Hendrix's grave is. My mood turns heavy; like many musicians, I feel deeply connected to him – and his death suddenly seems much more real to me. I guess because his music still lives on, I feel like he does too. I get out and slowly wander through the headstones, reading the names. After ten minutes of not finding the headstone, I wonder if I got the section wrong in my research. I scan the expansive cemetery, just trying to sense what the right direction might be. Over a small knoll, fifty yards in front of me, seems like the way. I crest the knoll and notice a headstone with lots of flowers surrounding it. My gut tells me to check it out. As I approach the grave, I know right away it's him by the engraving of a Stratocaster on the stone. I slow my approach, feeling each step, to honor this musician who has given me so much. And then I'm standing over the headstone. I think, *Here he is, wow.* I let out a big breath and really try to absorb the depth of his influence on me and that's he's actually gone. A wave of deep sadness washes over me – I hadn't excepted to feel this way. I read the inscription:

FOREVER IN OUR HEARTS
JAMES M.
"JIMI" HENDRIX
1942 –1970

Wanting to get closer to him, I lower myself on my haunches and reach out and run my fingers along the engraved letters of his name. "Hey, buddy," I say as my hand travels along the engraving of the Stratocaster. "Thanks for everything. Thanks for staying on me." I laugh a little at the truth of it. "Whatever happens, brother, I hope I can honor what you have given me." I close my eyes, feeling that growing strength in me, and then I sense more words wanting to come; I take a quick glance around to see if anybody is around. A sudden wind ruffles my hair.

"Dad, thanks for getting me here. You were right about everything. I guess I had to learn in my own way, right? It seems all my life I've been afraid of so many things. Afraid of not being as good as I hoped to be, remember? That's a tough one. It's better to live in hope than to find out I wasn't good enough. It's like I was afraid folks wouldn't see what's inside me – or that I wouldn't be able to show them, really show them, you know? To help them see the struggle of people and their dignity, too. Man, if I could do that..."

"You a friend of Jimi?" a woman's voice behind me asks, startling me. I jump up and turn around to find an elderly black woman, wearing a beautiful light-blue going-to-church-on-Sunday hat, looking curiously at me. She's holding a bouquet of gorgeous flowers.

"I'm sorry, ma'am. I didn't mean to bother..."

She interrupts me, "It's all right, son. Were you and

Jimi friends?" she asks gently.

"No, ma'am, but he was very important to me, his music..." I stop, feeling any words would be inadequate to describe his influence on my life.

She watches my eyes and says, "Jimi loved to play that guitar." Then she laughs and adds, "Used to sleep with it!"

I laugh with her, thinking I didn't know that. We stand there, in an introspective moment, looking down at the grave.

"Yup, he was a fine boy, respected his elders. He practiced all the time, you know, worked hard at it. He and his father were real close. He was quite a tap dancer, his father."

"My dad liked to dance the Twist!" I tell her. Feels good that Jimi and I had this in common. I wanted to find out how she knew Jimi, but I felt it would be intrusive to ask.

"Fine way to get the Spirit going," she adds, merrily.

"Definitely," I say, smiling. "Ma'am, can I ask you a question?"

"Sure."

"When Jimi was alone, you know, just with himself, what kind of music did he like to play?"

"Lot of things, but I mostly remember him playing the old blues like you find down south. I think Jimi felt the history of our race in it. Mm-hmm. The music traveled a long way, hasn't it? It's still out there. Needs to keep going, need to keep *that feeling* going."

At her powerful words, all the emotions in my soul rush up inside me. I try to will them down so as to not make her feel uncomfortable.

She watches me closely and then seems to come to a realization, "Do you play guitar, son?"

With that question, I can barely hold back my tears, so I stare down at the ground and answer quietly, "Yes, ma'am."

I raise my eyes and know she can see the thousands of miles on my heart.

"Have you found what you were looking for?" she asks me – the question that has been staring me in the face since Mississippi.

Something in me breathes suddenly, finally realizing the answer to her big question. "I think so, ma'am…I think so."

"Sooner or later, we catch up with ourselves," she says.

I nod humbly, knowing full well what she means.

"Now, you lay these flowers next to him for me." She hands me the bouquet, and I position it gently against the headstone. She makes the sign of the cross and silently mouths a short prayer. I bow my head in respect. After a moment, she says, "It was nice visiting with you, son."

"You too. Can I walk you back to your car?"

"That would be very nice. It's a bit far. I visited with a lot of folks before seeing Jimi."

"My pleasure." I extend the crook of my elbow so she can hold it, and we head slowly back to her car.

CHAPTER FORTY-NINE
Char Montgomery

Robert wakes up this morning and says we need to go to the cemetery. I know now to go along with whatever guidance he has. At the hotel elevator, I suggest we make a quick stop at a rental shop to get a small portable amplifier so he can play something to Hendrix. At which point, he says, "Forget the elevator," and bolts down the stairs!

A little while later, we pull up to an iron-grated archway that says *Greenwood Park Memorial – South Entrance.*

"This is it," I announce. I'm as nervous as a bee and doing my best to hide it from Robert.

"I think we got lost, Char. This is the south entrance. Shouldn't we go to the north entrance?"

"We can get there this way."

"You've been here before?" he inquires, surprised.

"I have." I find my mood turning solemn, which is what I always experience when I come here. We drive on the winding roads through the gravestones for a few minutes until I see the section marker. I pull up, turn the motor off, and sit quietly for a moment. Robert is staring hard out of the window at the headstones.

"Jimi is over there, isn't he?" I hear a super-heaviness in his ten-year-old voice.

"Yes, he is."

He turns, looking at me with those big brown eyes. "Should we go visit him?"

"Maybe we should wait for James to show up?" I ask.

"I think it's okay," he reassures me.

"Okay." Again, for me, it's "let go and let Robert." I learned back home, follow the signs – always.

We get out of the car and Robert grabs his guitar and amp from the backseat and we move slowly through the headstones and see up ahead one with an overabundance of flowers surrounding the stone. I hear "Purple Haze" in my mind. Invariably, I sense the presence of his music here. Robert reaches out, and I can feel his little hand vibrating as he holds my hand. We reach Jimi's grave, and both stare down at it for a long minute.

"Jimi must get kind of lonely," Robert says, sadness threaded through his voice.

"I'm sure people visit him a lot," I reply, trying to make him feel better. I begin to get concerned; it didn't occur to me that this might be upsetting for him.

"You think so?" he asks, hopefully.

"Definitely. That's why there are so many flowers here."

"He was only twenty-seven, you know. That's not very old."

"I know."

"Hi Jimi, I'm Robert, James Ryder's backup guitarist, I'm sure you have been listening to him – he is really good. I wanted you to know I practice a lot." He leans in towards the headstone as if hearing something, and then he turns to me. "Char, he says you should put your hand on his name and don't worry about anything."

I shake my head, blown away, thinking, *Jesus, now the kid is talking to Jimi. I'm in a world of magic, I guess. There is no turning back.*

"Okay, kiddo. I'm with you." I get down on my knees and place my hand across the engraved name on the stone, and Robert rests his hand over mine.

"We're with Jimi now, Char. He's not lonely."

CHAPTER FIFTY
James Ryder

After a nice walk through the cemetery, we arrive at her car. I didn't ask her any more questions about Jimi; it didn't feel right to push her.

"That's my car." She points to an immaculately kept light-blue Caprice. I open the driver's door and help her get behind the steering wheel and then close the door gently.

"Thanks," she says. There is such deep kindness about her. I feel so grateful I ran into her, and I know in my heart it wasn't an accident.

"My pleasure. It was nice meeting you, ma'am."

"You're a good boy. What's your name?"

"James Ryder."

She starts the engine.

"James Ryder! Like the sound of that!" she declares with a big smile on her face, a joyful merriment wrapped around my name.It makes me sense the real me inside. She holds me in her vision for a long moment, making sure I've received her unspoken message.

"Thanks again, ma'am." I truly hope she sees in my face and hears in my voice how much that means to me.

She pulls away, and as I watch her drive down the road, I say to myself, *Wow, it's amazing how one person can have such an effect on you.* I stroll over to the Corvette, thinking I will grab some lunch and circle back around to Hendrix's grave before I head down the road. As I open the driver's door, I get a vibe not to get in – not the first time I've had such instincts. Glancing around the cemetery, I see no one. I take a second sweep around and spot a flash of what looks to be a big black dog with a long black tail crest over the knoll where we came from. I figure it's just some local dog wandering in the cemetery. I decide to jump in the car and fire the 'Vette up.

CHAPTER FIFTY-ONE
Char Montgomery

As Robert and I stand over Jimi's headstone, I suddenly feel emotionally wiped out by all the pressure of putting the band together, visiting Hendrix again, and trying to find James. I am thankful Robert is here with me to keep my Spirit going.

I sense my Wolf-Sister's presence as she walks from behind me and sits back on her haunches next to Robert. She is supporting him in the same way she has done with me many times. Obviously, they have become fast friends. She turns her big head to look at me or behind me, I'm not sure.

I listen to Robert as he talks with Jimi. "See, Jimi, I brought my guitar. I wanted to show you what I learned. Did you know some of your stuff is pretty hard? So if it's not perfect, don't get mad, okay? This is one of my favorites. My mom likes it a lot too."

He begins to play "One Rainy Wish," a song Hendrix said came to him in a dream; it's truly beautiful.

After the first set of chords, I feel the lyrics surging up in me, and I can't hold them back. I sing out with a power I didn't know I had.

Suddenly, behind me, I hear a voice join me in the chorus. I turn quickly around, and James steps from behind a tree, his eyes happy, looking so much lighter than when I saw him last. My nerve-endings shoot up to the sky. Robert stops playing. I feel so apprehensive and embarrassed. I try to read his face to see if this is the biggest mistake I have ever made in my life.

"You're getting too good, partner," James tells Robert.

"Do you think Jimi liked it?" Robert asks as if they've been sitting here talking for hours.

"Absolutely. I am sure he really dug it." Then he rests his eyes on me, and I feel my heart jump – his smile gets even bigger. "And I don't think I have ever heard it sung prettier."

I'm standing there numb. I have no idea what to say or do, afraid to even look directly at him. I have never felt so vulnerable, exposed.

"I kind of got messed up on that third chord. Can you show me again?" Robert asks.

"Sure." James gets down on his haunches, taking the guitar and showing him how to finger the chord.

"Oh yeah, that's right. How's the road trip?"

"Got a lot of stories to tell you, partner."

"Cool!"

James whispers to Robert, "What's the matter with Char? She's really quiet."

Robert responds in a whisper, "Yeah, it's a little weird.

Did you know she is putting together a band?"

"I heard that. Do you think maybe she will let me try out?"

My head comes up quickly, and I gaze into the eyes of the lead guitarist I have been waiting so long for. "Really?" I ask, unbelieving, like a kid who finally gets the gift she has always wanted but can't believe it's really being given to her.

"Definitely!" James exclaims, his face glowing with excitement at what's ahead. "But I only have one condition."

"Anything!"

"When we get back to New York, we go on a date."

"I can do that, James Ryder, I can do that. It would be my honor." *And he wants to date me!* I yell inside my head. I've definitely shape-shifted into a sixteen-year-old!

"Just got to make two phone calls."

"Two phone calls?" I ask, confused.

"A little surprise. Oh, and Char, do you know there is a big black wolf that hangs out with you?"

Chapter Fifty-Two

Char Montgomery

I walk into the rehearsal room and find George and Cody waiting on me, standing by the window.

"Hey, guys. Sorry I'm late." I check their mood quickly to see how they will handle what's coming in right behind me.

"We were getting ready to split," George says, letting me know with his tone he's kidding.

"*He* was splitting, Char, not me," Cody counters. "Is there anyone in this building that will date a musician?"

I laugh, seeing nothing has changed in my absence. "Sorry, I had to pick up the guys at the airport." I feel them tense up at my mention of "the guys."

At that very moment, James, Sam, and John walk in the door. James and John hold guitar cases, and I see drumsticks sticking out of Sam's back pocket.

"Guys, this is James, Sam, and John. This is George and Cody."

George and Cody's faces go flat as they move away from the windows and stand directly opposite them. Its feels like a stand-off in the Old West. Tension fills the room. I'm not sure why, maybe they feel outnumbered.

They have dedicated months to this process, so I can understand them feeling that way. My instinct tells me to hang back.

James stands in front of George and Cody; he's so deeply in his feelings, so present, I can feel the essence of his vulnerability and openness.

"How you doing? Really sorry we were late," James says humbly, honoring that this is their space. I have told him how much these two cats have hung in with me.

Sam nods his head, offering a welcoming smile; the same feeling James extends – *we know we are late to the party, we aren't here to run you over.*

"Nice to meet you, y'all," John offers, in his Southern accent. He stands in a quiet, respectful manner that he embodies with every piece of his soul.

I have never heard Sam play or John sing, but if James says they are special, then I'm listening. Just in the handful of hours I have known them between picking them up at the airport and grabbing lunch, the pure authenticity they exude has blown me away – there is a realness about them. And the exchange between them and James at the airport is something I will never forget. I don't think I have ever seen three grown men so emotional with barely exchanging words. It was all unspoken – they're on a mission.

I see by George and Cody's body language they are a little defensive, on guard. George studies James like he is trying to remember James's face.

"You're James Ryder?" George inquires, as if he's seeing a unicorn.

James nods, smiling, eyes sparkling, appreciating the inference of George's tone.

"I've heard of *you*," George says, with the same serious expression I witnessed in the sax player's eyes at Grand Central Station – James is known and respected.

"I've heard of you, too, brother," James replies, extending his hand. "Honored to meet you." After he and George shake hands, James adds, "And you too, Cody."

When they're all done exchanging hand-shakes, I say, "James, why don't you show them what you've been working on."

"Okay," James says quietly, again treading very lightly.

I go behind my desk, and James and John open up their guitar cases. Sam approaches the drum-kit like he's moving towards an altar. When he identifies what kind of drums they are, he catches my eye and gives me a fist-salute with a big smile. I like it when Sam smiles. You know it means something. James had asked me to find the kind of Ludwig oversized drums that John Bonham used, and Red went crazy, calling all over town. Sam settles himself behind the drum kit and adjusts the placements of the drums and cymbals and tries a few licks. Right away, I can see the power he has.

Cody watches James closely, still a little pulled back.

James seems to be in some special zone, and I can see how connected he is to Sam and John.

Suddenly, the door opens, and the boss, Mr. Chandler, semi-charges in with his assistant and two other suited executives. Before I can say anything, he says sternly, "Just pretend were not here." His tone doesn't bode well.

"Okay. Whenever you're ready, guys," I tell the band, keeping the panic out of my voice. I catch James's attention, who reads my freaking-out eyes and sends me back a reassuring grin – his confidence level is in a totally different place. He doesn't seem fazed by the suits. He turns to George and Cody and says, "This is something Sam and I have been working on. Could we give it a try?"

George responds, "You go right ahead, man. We'll follow you."

Cody confirms with a thumbs-up, I can tell by his posture and attitude he's suddenly into the whole arrival of the rest of the band and the suits. Cody digs action!

James takes out a slide that I know Pops gave him, then turns to John who is standing beside him. "John, do the lyrics feel good to you?"

"I'm with you, brother. Worked on them on the plane," John confirms for him, and you can hear the affection he has for James. James told me and Robert great stories of how he met John and Sam and Pops. It's truly like some magical fairy tale. I feel proud that James has such a deep impact on folks so quickly.

He glances at Sam and says, "Sam, you count us in."

James leans into the mic and says, "This one is called, 'Angels on the Highway.'"

Sam hits his drumsticks together three times, and James lays down a series of haunting riffs using the slide that is right out of the Delta – the sound is so heavy, it's like a thirty-foot wave crashing over us; it just consumes the room. Sam enters, kicking the bass drum hard. It's actually as if the sound has taken on a 3D solidity in the air. It just hangs there and embraces me, like I could walk inside it. Slowly, in a natural evolution, the rhythm grows into a rock sound, James going into some complex fingering. It's as if James has captured the history of the evolution of the blues into rock in one sheet of music. He begins to sing in amazing harmony with John. I keep watching them closely because I swear it's one voice even though I know it isn't – each lyric has different emotions happening at the same time. Their harmony is like a painting with multiple layers, with new things to discover each time you experience it. I have never heard anything like this sound. The music draws me into a world of raw feeling – one I don't want to leave. It's magical and mysterious at the same time. George, who always stays cool, glances over at Cody, with an expression like, *Oh my God*, and he just brings in his bass guitar, laying down a rock-solid foundation – you would think they had been playing together for years. There is an obvious specialness to the band's sound that wasn't there with the other guitarists or drummer.

They finish and stand there, all a little stunned. No one says anything for a moment. My Wolf-Sister and I want to jump up and howl our hearts out, but I know my best move is to stay cool while I wait for the boss's reaction.

Mr. Chandler sits there contemplating the group for a long, painful moment, then abruptly gets up and says matter-of-factly, "Char, you better set up some studio time for these cats and start booking some dates. Good work."

"Thanks, Boss," I answer, matching his flatness. I don't think I have ever heard him use the word "cats" – which makes my Spirit soar to the heavens. It tells me he *hears* them.

"And stop calling me boss!" he yells at me.

"Yes, sir!"

They get up and head for the door, and I follow them. Mr. Chandler and the executives talk among themselves; they all seem enthusiastic about what they've heard. They pass through the door, and I give them a moment to get down the hallway, then I take a peek around the corner to see if they are out of ear-shot. The boss has lagged behind as his team moves away. I stop, so he doesn't see me.

I hear him whisper, "Wow!" Yessss!

I want to take a quick look so that I can witness his

expression, but I don't chance it. I pump my fist up and down in celebration and head back to the rehearsal room where the band is standing, waiting for me.

"I guess they liked us." George says, breaking the spell.

"You could say that, hoss!" I fire back and run around the room laughing in a victory dance.

CHAPTER FIFTY-THREE

James Ryder

Well, like the big boss ordered, we got into the recording studio – the next day! And for me, it was like living in the most joyful dream imaginable. All the music I had created over the years that I had kept hidden was now coming out with the best guys around. At the end of recording each track, we would all sit back behind the sound board and listen to the day's work. The whispers inside me were coming alive – I was finally honoring them. I couldn't believe that it was actually happening. My dad would have been so proud. Char put us with Scott, their best sound engineer at the company; he helped us create a sound that felt like the sixties but new at the same time and a few tracks with an ancient, stripped-down Mississippi Delta vibe. I knew how much this band meant to Char, and I was impressed how she let go, stood back, and allowed us to follow our own creativity. Once a day, she'd offer a suggestion that would just blow us away in its originality – opening up a deeper window into the track we were working on.

Where do I start about my four band mates? Man,

they just spoke my language right from the start. On each track, they added another layer to the music that was exactly what I heard in my head; it's as if they read my musical-mind, and then they would add a unique dimension that I hadn't thought of. That felt so special to me: to experience or merge with another musician's creativity. I just immediately trusted them. Sometimes I would wonder why I waited so long, but that brief thought slipped away in the pure creativity we all lived in for a month. I only shared this with Char, but during the month of recording, I felt my brothers and sisters from the Delta guiding and whispering to me. To honor them is everything to me.

With Sam, I had really only witnessed a small part of his gift on percussion; the more comfortable he got, the more his focused ferocity grew, and that inspired us all to match its level of intensity and insanity! I heard that he got a few offers from other record companies while we were recording. From what Char said, the response in his eyes would have scared a grizzly, and he had one answer: "I'm with James Ryder." When she relayed that to me, it was hard to keep it together – and I will never forget it.

The level of talent of George and Cody didn't surprise me, given Char's level of excellence – she would settle for nothing less than the best. My fears of being judged by other musicians, especially hard-core professionals like George and Cody, were unfounded. What happened was the opposite. Their support helped me every day in the studio; I felt they were truly *backing me up*. It was like I could soar with their rock-solid foundation to support me. My dad was right: "There will be other musicians that dig what you are trying to do." Because John and I had both lost our fathers, our singing together became very tight. We mixed it up; sometimes I would sing lead and sometimes he would, or we would sing the whole song in harmony.

At every turn, Char was there empowering us, and she got us anything we needed. Just her energy alone made me feel safe – she was a protector and I think musicians need that. Char gave Robert a taxi allowance so he could bolt over after school and be part of the recording sessions. Like me, the band adopted him, and when we got tired and overwhelmed, he was there to keep us smiling, and of course he played on one of the tracks to an audience of folks at the record company who he had befriended. Joan, his mom, was there that day and whispered to me and Char, "You made a difference in his life, I won't forget. And when are you guys getting married?" Char and I did go on that date, and then another, and another! She helped me so much to own who I am and to be proud of this gift I was given. She took a lot of teasing around the "record company camp-fire" for dating a musician! But in the end, Red cast the deciding vote. "When something makes sense, it just makes sense," she said. "Now, get back to work!" She was right – truly.

Char and I were *meant to be* from that first moment I saw her in the subway. We both knew it.

Seeing Char's Wolf-Sister was pretty mind-blowing, and I felt so grateful I could. The allegiance between them was a thing of beauty – a true sisterhood. While we were rehearsing, I would look up in the sound booth and see the big black wolf next to Char with her front paws on the sound board gazing down at us. It felt supportive, her magical presence kept me close to the mystery where I knew deeper levels of the music lay waiting. She was a gateway to that place. A few times, I felt like I heard her voice come into my head, saying, *You're safe, I'm here, I'm your friend, you can go deeper.* I told Char about this, and she looked at me surprised, saying, "She is talking to you? Wow! That's a big deal. It means she likes you a lot. I guess that means that's two of us!"

There were a few nights where I'd be in the studio by myself after everyone left, and I suddenly felt Char's Wolf-Sister sitting next to me, looking at me with those amazing amber eyes. There was such a wonderful vulnerability and softness about the energy she exuded; she taught me more about these emotional places. One time, it occurred to me to say something to her in my mind: *"I'm really glad you're here with me."* Then right away, I hear this female voice in my head. *"You're James Ryder, man who feels. I'm with you."*

That brought me to tears.

Once in a while, when we were laying down a track,

I would notice her standing amidst the band, and she'd let out a big howl and jump around in excitement; I came to realize that meant we had hit upon something that rang with the truth. One late night after she did this celebration-howling during a recording, instead of listening to what we put down, we were so tired we let it wait until the next day. When we played the tracks back, we could all hear a soft, deep resonate howl far in the background in perfect harmony with the music. All of us in the band looked at one another as if to say: What was that? We played it back and George said, "It's wolf howl!" Char and I smiled across the sound board at each other. I glanced around the room trying to sense her Sister's presence, and my attention felt pulled into the recording room where she was standing next to my guitar, looking at me with what felt like an expression of pure joy – having heard that she had contributed to the album.

I said to the group, "Works for me!"

The big boss, Mr. Chandler, only showed up one time during the recording sessions, which surprised me since I thought he would check in more. He arrived one night about 9:00 p.m. during a session that was going late. I saw him walk in the control booth and stand next to Char, who was sitting with Scott at the sound board. His tie was loosened, and he appeared more relaxed than usual when I passed him in the hall. He watched us for about a minute, kind of narrowing his eyes, nodded his head a few times, leaned down and whispered something in Char's ear, and then walked out. Char looked stunned, like a deer caught in the headlights. We all stopped playing, it was that alarming. She came down to us in the studio, a little dazed. We asked what was wrong.

"Far out," she told us, sounding spacey.

Cody asked, "Far out?"

"That's what the boss whispered to me in this super-relaxed, excited voice: 'Far out,' she repeated, mimicking Mr. Chandler's laid-back, passionate tone.

George chimed in, "That's a good thing, right?"

She took us all in for a moment, I think to show us that what she was about to share was important. "I just never thought I would hear those two words come out of him. When he hired me to create the band, I know now that's what he wanted, that was *his dream:* To walk in here one late night and see the band recording and to say those words that were locked away somewhere inside of him…it was like the twenty-five-year-old cat that started this record company with a few thousand bucks and a dream showed up. Wow."

We all saw in that moment how much it meant to Char to live up to the boss's belief in her and also, maybe, to help him get back to his original mission when he first started the company.

She went from one band member to the next with those serious Wolf eyes, letting us know we *mattered,* and said simply in this humble voice with her hand flat against her heart, "Thank you, guys. Thank you." And then she walked back to the sound booth.

We didn't say anything; but we just caught one another's eye, understanding what we owed Char and Mr. Chandler for this chance.

After we cut the album, Char went on a rampage across the country, making sure every disc-jockey and radio station from Maine to California was playing our music. She would never say anything to me, but from what I picked up from people talking in the hallways, she was a crazy person and would not take no for an answer – bringing out her full Montana Champion Bronc Riding personality, and with her Wolf-Sister along – well, who had a chance?

We went on tour for six months around the country, playing all sizes of venues from one hundred to five hundred people. Like Pops taught me, music is giving something away to folks, and each night this was always in my heart. I conveyed Pops's thoughts to John because it really mirrored what his dad taught him. Every night on stage, there would be one moment when John and I would exchange a long glance, nodding to each other. I know both of us were experiencing the exact same feeling – gratitude to share with folks, to maybe lift them up a little, to show them they weren't alone in their struggle or sadness. When I get to the end of my days, I will remember those little moments with John. Also, I never told anyone, but every so often I felt the presence of Hendrix – once, I thought I saw him in the audience, grinning up at me. I'm probably not the first musician who has imagined that. The nightmares stopped, and now of course I know it was him trying to help me from the other side. *I hope with all my heart I have honored him.* George and Sam became really tight on the road. Like me, Sam is a loner, and I'm glad he found a friend. Cody kept us all light and laughing when we were dead tired and had to get on the road to the next club.

When we moved through Mississippi, I took John and Char with me to visit Pops. John understood right away everything about the Delta, and the day we said goodbye to Pops, driving the rent-a-car down the road, he turned to me, with eyes filled and whispered, "Thank you, brother." He was honored to *see the root of all of it* – as he called it.

Pops adopted Char right away, and they spent a lot of time whispering together. She brought out a sweet part of him – I didn't know the old man had it in him! Finally, I said, "What are you two always going on about?" I was met with his usual gruffness, "Why aren't you practicing? Don't get too uppity with yourself." The funniest and most special moment was when he told her, "Charlotte, is that big black wolf that stays close to you hungry? We can fix her up something." He called her Charlotte; he said that's the name God gave her, and he was sticking to it.

One night on the porch, John and I got out our guitars and played a few songs off the album for Pops – one in harmony, and one John did by himself. I really wanted Pops to hear John's voice – it was as pure and emotional as ever. Truly, the earth was in his voice. After we finished, Pops stared at John, sort of scrutinizing him, then asked him, "Boy, your people from around these parts?"

I lowered my eyes to the ground, so I wouldn't embarrass myself with the tears I was trying to hold back. John looked at the old man, his eyes filling. He knew what Pops was saying and said, "No, sir, but it sure does feel like where my Daddy came from back in the mountains." Pops gave him one of his "Mm-hmms" – meaning he could see the truth.

When we were walking to the car to leave, Pops called after me, "Son?" I turned around, Char and John, a few steps in front of me, turned too. He was standing on the porch and spoke to me across the tall Delta grass, "Everyone heard that music you playing, and you made us all proud."

I knew who he meant by "everyone." I stood there frozen, so blown away, not sure what to do or say. There is no greater honor for me than to make the *other five* musicians in the woods proud of me. I heard Char behind me crying; seconds later, she dashed by me, ran up to Pops and hugged him, and then turned around quickly and ran towards the car, the tears streaking her face.

"Charlotte, you take care of these boys, you hear?"

he called after her.

She nodded adamantly, waving goodbye.

"And keep that Wolf close, that's magic you got there."

Tonight, we've arrived back home in New York and the destination we have been driving toward – a big show at the Beacon Theatre. For me, it's a special moment because this is the place I have been hiding from for so many years, and with Pops's help, *I know I don't have to hide anymore.*

CHAPTER FIFTY-FOUR
Char Montgomery

We're in the Green Room at the Beacon in New York waiting to go on; the dressing room is small and full of character, unlike the blandness of contemporary ones I've been in. I can hear the big crowd buzzing in the distance, matching my energy. I keep trying to remember to breathe. I'm wearing my special, beaded-fringed deer-skin jacket to honor this moment, my thick hair in full blown-out-of-control mode, falling down my back. The door opens, and Chris, an old friend and the stage manager wearing headphones and a mic, comes in.

"Char, five minutes," he alerts us.

"Okay." The butterflies just amped up to full capacity in my stomach – tonight is important – this is New York.

Chris announces, so happy for me, "You're sold out! Full capacity – three thousand in the audience!"

"Really!?" I respond, surprised, feeling like a little kid.

Chris laughs. He totally gets that this gig is very important to me. "You got a winner, rodeo-girl! Just get me a signed something! Cool?"

"You got it, hoss!" We exchange veteran looks, knowing how hard it is to have a successful band.

I turn around to find the band focused, checking their instruments, getting their game face on. Over the last six months, with each show they just kept getting tighter and tighter in their sound. It was wonderful to be part of it and witness the overwhelming love from the audience and their connection to the songs on the album – at each stop, they would sing along.

I have been part of so many bands and seen how, after a time, they stop being friends; not these cats. They are like brothers – sharing a deep bond on and off stage. Even though James is the leader, never for one moment did I see him try to dominate or control. What I really loved was his wish that John sing lead on four out of the twelve tracks we cut for the album. Robert is with us tonight – this is the first time he will see the band on stage. I'm not sure if he's my adopted little brother or some sort of Spirit Guide! Bottom-line: without him, this might not have happened. My Wolf-Sister stayed close to me through this whole journey, lending me her power. This is traditional in my lineage – to be in partnership. And, as always, it makes a huge difference – when she sees me fading, getting emotionally wiped out from launching the band, she helps me channel her never-back-down fierceness, and I bounce back. I go, she goes – forever.

"All right, guys" I say, "five minutes. Gather around for a minute. You all have done a great job. This is the band I've imagined all my life! The album is selling like crazy, the tour went great. New York! We made it! Now, don't let the fact that every music critic in the free world is sitting out there worry you."

"Thanks, Char, we really appreciate you mentioning that," George quips. He's looking pretty dapper tonight with a dark suit and tie – very bebop. Cody brought out his killer threads of black leather pants and brown velvet shirt. Sam is in jeans with a pressed, black, Western-style shirt with black pearl buttons. John finally gave into wearing the brown leather blazer I gifted him; I know pretty much every single dollar he makes goes back to his family, so I have tried to take care of him. James went with his trademark dark blue shirt and jeans with brown-leather and silver conch belt. My Wolf-Sister is sitting next to him, resting against his leg, supporting him. I catch his eye and press my hand against my right thigh, meaning *do you feel her?* He grins and puts his hand over his heart. My Sister looks focused, radiating calm. She and James have become very close; it seems she's always by his side, giving him a doorway to deeper creativity. Their immediate kinship means more than I can say – that the man I love can actually see and feel her is beyond anything I could have wished for.

"Does anybody need anything?" I ask.

Everyone gives me the *we're cool* signal. "All right! Here we go! Let's do it."

James speaks up, "Guys, before we go on, I have little announcement. Well, first, do you cats own a suit or something?"

"A suit?" Cody, always the first to speak up, asks, confused.

George says, "How's this?" indicating what's he wearing.

"Looks good," James says, confirming George's look. "Yeah, I need four best men. The other day, Char *told* me we better get hitched or there was going to be trouble back in Big Sky Country with her folks. Something about being lassoed and dragged through prickly bushes."

I yell, "What! I never you told you that!"

"That's the way I remember it. Robert will back me up."

Robert, of course, backs him up, "Char, that's pretty much what you said. I was listening."

All the guys gather around congratulating us.

I chirp in, "And Cody, stay away from Red at the wedding. You've both been warned! My staff does not date musicians! You're horrible people!"

"Char, she kind of smiled at me the other day. I think it's a sign!" Cody pleads, flashing that sexy grin that had girls following the tour bus across the country.

George yells, "Let's do it! This one is for Char and James!" They head out the door. Sam and John stop, looking back at James, who hasn't moved.

"You coming?" Sam asks, showing a little concern. They always head to the stage together as a group – it's a ritual.

"I'll be right behind you, brother," James responds.

John asks, "You, okay?"

"Absolutely," James says, smiling easily to reassure him; he seems more in his soul each day. I know how much it meant for him to invite Sam and John on this journey, to give them a place to express their gifts.

John, reading his brother's energy and seeing everything is fine, says, "All right, we'll see you out there."

The band leaves, shutting the door behind them.

James says to Robert, "This is it, partner. What do you think?"

"Time to rock and roll!" Robert is bouncing out of his skin; this tough New York City kid is digging the whole concert process. He's truly in heaven! He's already run out of the dressing room a few times to check the crowd and then bolted back to report, "There are a lot of people out there!"

James sits down and gets at Robert's height, his face turning very serious, and says, "Listen to me, partner.."

Robert quiets down, registering his teacher and brother's seriousness.

"This..." James waves around the room, out towards the audience, and to a stack of the band's albums sitting in a box. "...would not have happened without *you*. I would not be sitting here right now without *you*. You are part of the band – always. Okay, Backup?"

The tears start to form in Robert's eyes. In the

months I have known him, I have never seen him cry. James grabs him in a long hug.

"Now, I have to talk to Char for a minute. Can you go ahead of me? I'll see you by the stage. And you saw your mom sitting in the first row, right?"

Robert wipes the tears from his eyes, "Yup, I waved at her."

"I told her she could come backstage, but she said, 'Nope, I want to be a fan tonight!' You got your V.I.P. pass?"

"Right here." He picks up the pass hanging around his neck. "See, Char put my name on it, 'James's Backup.'"

James chuckles. "Char's got everything covered, as always. Okay, see you out there."

I walk Robert over to the door, opening it to see media, tech, and support people running hurriedly around in the hallway.

I spot Chris and call out to him. "Chris."

"What's up?"

"Can you take my buddy here up to the stage?" Robert waves at James through the open door.

"No problem." He looks down at Robert and says, "You ready, Backup?"

I hear Robert say to him, "You're the boss around here, huh?"

"Pretty much. Char told me reserve a concert date for you in about ten years."

"That's sounds about right," Robert answers totally seriously, like there is no doubt!

They walk off, yakking away – Robert has made another friend.

I close the door and turn to find James still pretty emotional after talking to Robert.

"Sit down for a second, honey," he says, so I sit across from him, knees touching, and he reaches out and holds my hands. "Listen, I just wanted to tell you…" he turns his head to the side, something I have learned he will do when emotion is overtaking him. I am trying to keep my stuff together too. I don't know what it is about playing in New York – it makes everything more charged. He continues, "…Thanks for believing in me. It's everything to me…" He pats his chest twice, bowing his head. "… Everything."

The tears start to fall down my cheeks, I can't hold them back anymore, especially because the moment I have been waiting for, for so many years, is upon me.

"You're an easy person to believe in, my love. Thanks for trusting me. I'm so grateful we found each other." I reach out and hug him, feeling the powerful connected energy that is always there between us.

"I guess it's *time*," he says, a beautiful soft smile on his handsome face.

I look at my lead guitarist, my soon-to-be husband, and say, "Yes, it is." But in this moment, I don't mean getting on stage quite yet – *one last thing to do*. I stand up, wiping the tears from my face, pulling myself together, take out a key, and go over to unlock the closet door where *my Talisman* is waiting. My Wolf-Sister trails next to me, her amber eyes shining with anticipation; this is a big moment for her also. I reach in, pick up the worn, rectangular, black guitar case, and rest it flat on my palms; as I turn to James, he immediately stands up, sensing this is something important. He's never seen the guitar case. After we got back to New York from Seattle, I put it away in a special place. I have rehearsed this moment so many times in my mind, and it's more powerful than I could have ever imagined it. My Wolf-Sister stands next to me – her mood excited, open, emotional. She was the one who led me to my talisman. When I stood up at that special music auction all those years ago, she told me, "No matter what it costs..." I believed in her like she has always believed in me – for we are one. I look across the room at James, raising my chin in fierce pride, and announce, "I am Char Montgomery, adopted granddaughter of the great Crow nation, blood-sister to the Wolf-People. This is for you, James Ryder. A Ho." I reach out my arms, presenting the case to him.

James hesitates for a second, caught off guard by my solemn words. He takes the case gently from me, his gaze running over its length and black leather surface and looks up at me, studying my eyes. I think he's trying to find a clue to what's this is about.

I place my hand softly on top of the case and say, "I

waited a long time to find the right person to give this to. I knew that if I started with *this*...with the feeling I had for what's inside, if I had faith, that person would show up."

"Char, baby, what's in here?" he asks, nervously, sensing there could be something ominous inside.

"I know he would have wanted you to have it." I feel the tears streaming down my face, but I don't move to wipe them away. My Wolf-Sister and I stand there proudly – the sisterhood of the wolf. Not for one second do I hold anything back. I have never felt safer with another human being – I know this special man honors my soul.

"Should I open it?" James asks, tentatively, respectfully.

I nod firmly and say, "A Ho." He understands this expression.

James lays the case down on the long table under the dressing room lights and checks with me once more to make *sure* he should open it.

I nod my head again, reassuring him, smiling deeply from my heart, so excited to see his reaction.

He clicks open the locks and lifts the cover and stares down, trying to comprehend what he is seeing inside the guitar case. I feel my Wolf-Sister lift her head to the ceiling and let out two enormous howls in celebration, "ARH-WOOOOOO... ARH-WOOOOOO."

On the upper inside-cover of the case in white lettering is spelled: JIMI HENDRIX. Resting inside is one of Jimi Hendrix's personal Fender Stratocaster guitars. James squints his eyes hard, trying to absorb the unimaginable for any guitarist – the holy grail.

"Char, is this...?" he asks, I think needing me to confirm he's not dreaming.

"It is, and it's for you!"

James is stunned, shaking his head back and forth, trying to understand; he starts to choke up, stuttering, "Char, what...I don't understand...where did you..."

"You help people hear what's inside of them. The music lives in each one of us, and you show us how to find it, James Ryder. I am honored to be part of it. Please accept this gift."

He grabs me in a hug, holding me tight against him. I feel all the love I have for this man pouring into him.

We come apart, and he looks down at Jimi's guitar, reaching out to touch it with his fingers as if it's the most sacred of objects.

The Stratocaster seems to shine a white light up at us.

"It's so beautiful," James tells me in awe.

"I thought you might like to play it here in New York on this special night. I feel that's what he would have wanted."

"Really?!"

"Definitely!"

James reaches into the case. "Hey, pal," he says, and

lifts the guitar very carefully out, holding it upright to take a closer look, his eyes traveling the length of the guitar, taking in every inch. Then he puts the strap slowly over his head, resting his right palm against the strings, pressing the guitar against his body, closing his eyes; I'm sure he's trying to sense Hendrix's energy.

A wonderful peacefulness spreads over James's face. He opens his eyes, resting them on me, and shares in a quiet wistful voice, "He never gave up on me. His song, 'Are You Experienced' haunted me for so long but I knew it was his way of reminding me. I am so grateful."

"He was looking after you."

"He was, Char Montgomery, he was. And it's time to thank him." James tilts his head to the heavens and says with an inner strength threaded through his voice, reflecting his long journey, "This one's for you, Jimi."

With eyes shining with excitement, he looks at me and then down at my Wolf-Sister and asks, "Is the Sisterhood ready?"

My Sister and I let out a joint deep, joyous howl, ARH-WOOOOOOOOOOO.

"I love you both very much." He reaches out and give me a final hug, then turns and charges out the door into the hallway, holding Jimi's Stratocaster tight to his body. Chris, who's been waiting in the corridor, spots him and cues the announcer through his headset. I can hear the announcer's voice on the loudspeaker: "LADIES AND GENTLEMEN..." In a half-run, like a knife cutting through the air, James flashes down the packed corridor; people quickly move aside, staring at him as he passes. I'm right behind him, my whole body vibrating, my Wolf-Sister running next to me, so excited that we have arrived. He bounds up the steps to the stage, a dark seriousness now in his eyes, and sees his backup, Robert, beaming at him. James gives him a giant grin and raises his fist in front of his chest in a traditional salute. Robert returns it, pumping his fist, pride for his teacher bursting from every inch of him – the brotherhood of the guitar.

James runs on stage, extending the fist-salute to his band members who all return it; each one of them so happy to be part of the band. They are super-focused and relaxed at the same time, connecting and locking in with their front man – the path without words.

The announcer yells: "DELTA BLUE!!!" and at that exact moment, James stops center-stage and rips out a series of deep, resonant chords that echo over and over across the concert hall – it's like thunder that goes on and on and you want it to never end because its power comes inside you – you are the thunder. The crowd goes wild. The band bursts in. The sound is powerful, earthy, deep with feeling. James stands still, tearing out each chord in incredible intensity, his whole being one with the guitar. He holds the finishing notes to the brief opening number, bending the strings, leaning back, eyes closed, lost in his playing, squeezing the sound out of Jimi's Stratocaster as it travels in waves of rich tones across the crowd into the darkness. The audience roar is deafening.

Robert's little arms are in the air as he yells at his brother. My Wolf-Sister stands beside me, a *knowing* flowing from her amber eyes; she *saw* from the beginning where we would end up. She has always been ahead of me – leading the way.

My friends, how does anyone truly explain with words when the dream you have lived with since you were a little girl comes true right in front of you? There are no words – only the deepest joy. My fervent wish for you is your dream will *also* come true – never, ever stop believing.

James steps over to the mic and says with that deep kindness that lives inside him, "We're Delta Blue. Thank you for coming tonight. My brothers and I are truly grateful. This one is called 'Never Forget Where You Came From.' It's for those who kept the music alive."

CHAPTER FIFTY- FIVE
James Ryder

I reach down and plug into my small portable amp, the familiar stone pillars behind me. Char and Robert sit quietly on a low wall, understanding this *honoring* – next to them is a beautiful black wolf, the mysteries of the world in her amber eyes. I stand on my old spot, the tightly grouped buildings of Wall Street around me, and I begin to play my electric guitar, feeling myself move into that special place of stillness. I stare straight ahead into the far distance, connecting with my brothers and sisters from the Delta; my lone guitar chords echoing from here to the past. I'm on the other side of the crossroads now, brothers and sisters, setting free the whispers inside me.

THE END

AFTERWORD

The journey of creating *The Lead Guitarist & The Sisterhood of the Wolf* has a long history. I thought you might find it a powerful story about never giving up. Many of my clients who come on spiritual retreats are challenged with allowing their dreams, talents, and gifts to come out and be realized. I hope that my inner-journey behind the publishing of the book might be encouraging to you. Transparency!

First, PLEASE DON'T READ ANY FURTHER IF YOU HAVE NOT READ THE BOOK!! I am going to reveal some secrets about the book in this Afterword that will ruin the story for you! That's the last thing I want!

In the mid-eighties, when I was still acting, my longtime business coach, David Dowd, suggested I write a movie to act in based on some writing I had shown him. At first, I thought that was crazy. I didn't know anything about writing a movie! But I trusted David 100 per cent, so I started to study with the late Syd Field who, at the time, was the guru of screenwriting. During this time, I lost my older brother, Robert, and a few days after the funeral for some reason, I just began writing a screen-play. I have always felt he left me his determination. I would wake up every morning at 7:00 a.m., have a cup of coffee, and write for twelve hours straight until 7:00 p.m.! I felt at home in writing. It took six weeks, and I called the movie *The Lead Guitarist* and wrote the part of James Ryder for myself! (Please forgive me for writing him as handsome!) As I was building the scenes in the screenplay, I'd close my eyes and let the music of Robert Johnson and Jimi Hendrix create the next moment in the story of James Ryder and Char Montgomery. The music was the tour bus to their journey! It was while writing the Mississippi scenes that I had my first experience of vividly remembering a past life. I was suddenly transported back to the Delta during those times of persecution; I recollect I started to cry very hard with the realization that I had been there. I believe this was when my clairvoyance opened up to a broader level. I felt so grateful that those memories came through and I could honor the message of "a lot of folks left us too early to keep the music alive."

At first, the screenplay received serious attention and interest from Hollywood but was not "greenlighted." I had let go of the idea of acting in it and made the development of the movie my number-one priority. I went on to write seven more screenplays! Over the years, I kept working on The Lead Guitarist, and with each rewrite, it got more powerful. Among all my writing, the script was special to me. When I had stage IV throat cancer and was down to twenty percent survival rate, I made of list of eight things I wanted to accomplish if I survived. Well, as you can see, I did make it! I achieved seven of those things on the list very quickly. The last one remaining was seeing *The Lead Guitarist* made into a movie.

In the last few years, as I have gotten older, I've come to accept that the movie wasn't going to happen. I had made a lot of good runs at it with some great supporters along the way. You don't have to be in the movie business to know how incredibly difficult it is to get a film made, especially if you're no longer part of the "industry."

After the success of my second book, *The Shaman & His Daughter*, one day it occurred to me, I could adapt the screenplay of *The Lead Guitarist* into a novel! Why this idea-light didn't get turned on for over thirty years, you got me! I finally realized the important thing was that the story is told, no matter what the medium. Sometimes we have to let go of the original vision or dream and improvise! That is an enormous takeaway – please hear it! But, and this is a big "but," I really didn't want to make the personal writing journey to adapt it. I had lived with the screenplay for over three decades and through a half-dozen drafts. Also, I wasn't totally sure I had the writing chops to do it; it just felt too daunting, or maybe I was just lazy – any of these will do for an excuse! So, after some long thought, I did something that in the moment felt brave: I posted on three free-lance sites, looking for a ghostwriter or co-author! Crazy, right? And this from the writer who has sold thousands of books! But for me, it was important to get the story out there. I could drop my ego and let someone else adapt it from the screenplay. You could say I was let-ting go and looking at the big picture. Then a very strange thing happened: within one minute after hitting the button to post the third ad, I sat down and wrote the first seventeen pages of the book! It just came out of nowhere. It was like a beautiful, creative muse landed on the roof of my red-brick house here in Sedona!

After I finished the book, there was an inquiry I felt was important to make: Why did I start writing sud-denly? My coach, David Dowd, taught me "you have to get on the field and get visible, and things have a way of happening." By posting the ads, I got visible. Also, I think that the act of placing those ads was a way of exploring the possibility, another David-teaching. And when you do that, it creates an opening that built a land-ing-pad for the creative muse! Why is this important? The road to creating a breakthrough is not always clear. But what is super-clear is to take action. Here on per-sonal growth retreats, I teach it as "following the expres-sions of Divinity or Spirit." You don't have to understand the direction Divinity is pointing – only follow it! Divinity said, "Let go and post those ads."

So right away, I contacted my writing coach and editor to arrange a date on his editing schedule. I wrote another sixty pages pretty quickly, but then suddenly the flow of the writing stopped cold – and I mean, hard-core frozen! For several weeks, I was in the middle of an arena of giant RESISTANT-GLADIATORS trying to take me out; I lost count of how many times I considered giving up on the book. I just couldn't find a consistency in the writing process or the narrative voice, what is called a writer's "voice." There were some real strange happenings; I would wake up, adamantly planning to write, but nothing would flow out, and I'd say in agonizing frustration, That's it, I'm shelving it for good! And then at 6:00 p.m. the same day, I'd write five pages that had glimmers of my voice. It was a little schizoid and getting to me! On September 9th (documented on my Instagram), I was super stuck, sitting in front of the PC, and I decided I would just not get up from my chair until I figured out the next sentence. I fully embraced the uncomfortableness (it felt like suffering). I went inside myself, being patient, believing I could do it, and suddenly I broke through! The Greg-writing-voice started to come back.

What brought me across the finish line was introducing the Wolf into the story. It's another example of "following the expressions of Divinity or Spirit." When I published *The Shaman & His Daughter* and I was engaging in Facebook groups, I noticed how popular wolves were. I thought it might be cool in my next writing project to create a story that talked about the Wolf-People, never thinking it would be *The Lead Guitarist & The Sisterhood of The Wolf*! Then I stumbled across the great photo of a black wolf taken by Shari Jardina called "Amber." The Wolf's fierce energy and how she was peeking between the trees spoke to my soul as I know it does with many people. Then, given my thirty-five years of being grounded in shamanism, Native American medicine work, and animal totems, it just occurred to me to explore Char having a Wolf totem, especially since she was from the Northern Plains and was adopted by a Crow elder. Introducing the Wolf to the story was the key to fully refinding the Greg-writing-voice. It reminded me of who I am now – a shamanic healer, a medicine person. You see, I'm a very different person now than when I first wrote the screenplay all those thirty-odd years ago. I really couldn't write from the Old Greg perspective, which I now see is what I was trying to do and why I got stuck. But I could bridge the two! The Old Greg and the New Greg! That's when the writing of the book really started to fly. After that, I never looked back, and it kept flowing without effort. The fact the book actually exists is unreal for me and something I feel very proud of.

Some cool things about the book: You have to remember, it was written before the explosion of the Seattle scene with Pearl Jam, Soundgarden, Alice in

Chains, and Stone Temple Pilots. Was that the music I heard in my head when I wrote the screenplay? You could say it was in the next neighborhood! There are certain tracks from each one of these groups that I could point to that reflect the sound. Perhaps one that stands out is when Soundgarden and Pearl Jam teamed up to create the album, *Temple of the Dog*, especially the song "Hunger Strike" with both Chris Cornell and Eddie Vedder doing vocals.

Somewhere in the late nineties at a Tower Records listening station, I stumbled onto an album by Kelly Joe Phelps, considered by many musicians the premier slide-guitar player in the world. When I put those headphones on and heard his album, *Lead Me On*, I couldn't believe it – it was exactly what I heard in my head when James is playing guitar by himself in his room and music that is referenced later in the book when I write about the stripped-down Delta tunes that are created by James's band for their album. I found out what venue Kelly Joe was playing at and FedExed him the screenplay. I subsequently met with him a half-dozen times over the years at his gigs. His words about the script meant so much to me: "You nailed it!"

It was only two years ago that I came across a musician whose music or way of playing I felt embodied the spirit of James Ryder. I was watching the Showtime series called *Roadies*, and in one episode, a guest musician was doing a sound-check, and what I witnessed blew me away. That cat was Jordan Cook, aka Reignwolf (his band's name doesn't have anything to do with my putting a wolf in this story!). I invite you to look him up on YouTube! It's "heavy." He is truly out of his body and plays with pure abandon.

I hope this backstory of the book has given you a peek inside one author's creative process. Bottom line: Follow the breadcrumbs of Spirit!

ACKNOWLEDGMENTS

The first person I'd like to thank is Mary Brancato-Larson, who sat with me in a variety of restaurants and listened very patiently and enthusiastically as I read pages from the original screenplay; her support was crucial on my first writing journey – over thirty years ago!

Of course, many thanks to my business coach of thirty-four years, David Dowd, the maniac who has kept telling me, "You are a writer – write!"

I want to thank the late Egon Dumler, my mentor and entertainment attorney of many years, who always stood by me and believed in the screenplay. He saw something in me – I hope I have honored him.

A continued thank you to Mark Chimsky, my writing coach and editor, for understanding my "voice."

To my brothers and sisters in the Mississippi Delta and to all the musicians that came from there, thank you for helping me remember to "Never forget where you came from."

With each writing project, I lean on specific inspiration. This is an element I talk about with retreat clients – find partners. It can be a quote, a video, a movie, a book, a song, or even memories. In this case, it was three cats on Instagram and YouTube. The most important of the three was David Goggins, an ex-Navy SEAL and ultramarathoner. He has one message – to paraphrase: "Embrace suffering! Stop thinking that moving forward or creating a breakthrough will happen any other way." Then Jocko Willink, another ex-Navy SEAL, and Gary Vaynerchuck ("Garyvee"). I want to thank all of them for keeping me going and facing the uncomfortable and getting after it! You guys made a difference – period.

I want to thank Led Zeppelin. I hope this book and *The Shaman & His Daughter* reflect my gratitude for their powerful and continual inspiration and for being an important part of the fabric of my life!

Back 38 years ago when I was using and drinking, Tommy Shaw of Styx's song *Fooling Yourself (The Angry Young Man)*, helped me to stay alive. I finally get a chance in this book about rock & roll to say, "Thank you, brother, thank you."

To Jimmy Page, Eric Clapton, Jeff Beck and the great guitarists of our time, thank you so much for your creativity and the joy you have brought me.

I thank the great Crow nation of the Northern Plains for their whispers during the writing of this book. I hope I have honored them. My heart is full. A Ho.

My deepest thanks to Shari Jardina for giving me permission to use her photograph of the special black wolf titled "Amber." I hope with all my heart that I have honored the Wolf-People and the energy and sacred partnership of animal totems in the writing,especially my relationship with my Panther-Brother.

I like to acknowledge and thank the artist, Sawyer Fredericks (Voice Winner) and the wonderful film, "Songcatcher" directed by Maggie Greenwald (especially the scene with Iris DeMent) for inspiring me to take the character of "John" to a deeper level.

Thanks to Anugito, my graphic designer, for creating the cover, which spoke to my heart so deeply. And thanks to Kelsey Erin Sky for coming up with the idea.

Nothing I achieve is without my deep partnership with the Rock-, Tree-, and Plant-People and the Old Ones. I say to you, A Ho.

To friends who have supported me on my writing journey, I say thank you: Richard Barber, Joe Lair, Bill Minard, Marc Sterling, Siobhan Danreis, Dawn Newland, Cris Crago.

So many folks over the years tried their very best to get the movie made, and I want to thank all of them from the bottom of my heart. Who knows, maybe the book will lead to the movie!

I send gratitude to my brother Robert (Sam) for leaving me a great gift in the ongoing question: "So what are we going to do *now*?

Most importantly, I want to express my gratitude to my mother, who was a great storyteller and was always there for me during the writing of the screenplay. This special story would not have been told without her support. I will not retreat from this. "I love you, and I finally did it!"

To my Angel-Girl, you are my heart. And to AMB, you are inside every word I write.

As I close these acknowledgments, something has dawned on me: I want to thank one of my best friends – my writing! It really is like a friend to me and has brought me the deepest joy. I am so grateful.

Please Leave A Review On Amazon For
The Lead Guitarist & The Sisterhood of the Wolf

Also by Gregory Drambour: The Shaman &His Daughter

"70 Five Star Amazon USA/UK Reviews"

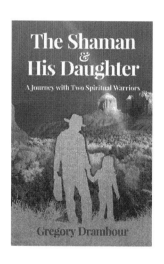

Do you struggle to hear your inner wisdom? Discover the power to know your inner-voice and act on it without hesitation.

Are you over-thinking? Are you experiencing emotional pain that you can't process? Gregory Drambour is a master shamanic healer and spiritual teacher with 35 years' experience empowering over 12,000 clients to a better understanding of the code of the spiritual warrior. Now he's sharing his wisdom with you through these powerful parables.

The Shaman & His Daughter contains 18 short stories that explore the special bond between a heartbroken father and his daughter, Angel-Girl. Through these tender tales you'll learn how Spirit can speak to you in times of darkness and expand your ability to heal your life.

In *The Shaman & His Daughter*, you'll discover:
- Inspiring lessons from a child raised to be a spiritual warrior and healer
- Wisdom that will guide you through your pain
- Simple practices to still your spirit and listen to the answers within
- How to trust your intuition and move toward healing
- How the path of the shaman can lead to a fulfilled life, and much, much more!

The Shaman & His Daughter is a moving educational book. If you like stories of inner strength, spiritual warriors in-training, and the beauty of a powerful father/daughter bond, then you'll love Gregory Drambour's inspiring saga.

Buy *The Shaman & His Daughter*
to heal your life today!

Paperback: $14.95 • ISBN: 0-978-1973836599
Ebook: $2.95
Available on Amazon, iBook, Barnes & Noble
Amazon link: https://tinyurl.com/shamandaughter

Excerpt from The Shaman & His Daughter:

CHAPTER ONE

The Fairy People
(Angel-Girl at five years old)

The world felt like it ended for me three years ago when my wife Shyheart was killed in a car accident. In that moment I truly wanted it to end so I could get to the afterlife and be with my soulmate and best friend. My life as a shamanic healer and spiritual teacher was put to the ultimate test.

The waves of pain and horror from losing her have begun to lessen over time. Perhaps it's because I have become really good at knowing what can distract me so that I'm not swimming around in sorrow. The list is short: writing, working with clients in my shamanic practice, and being with our special five-year-old daughter. Angel-Girl really doesn't remember her mother. I envy her that in some strange way, but I know she feels her mother. That's just who my daughter is, someone who feels deeply.

The sadness wave is definitely looming out there today on what would have been our twelfth wedding anniversary. I sit in my home office, watched over by the red rocks of Sedona, doing my best to distract myself by working on the weekly spiritual newsletter to my subscribers. The Danish teak desk I sit at always comforts me. There's something about its organic quality that resonates with my soul. What a challenge it was all those years ago to give myself permission to spend the money on such a thing of beauty. It was a gift to myself on my twenty-fifth sobriety anniversary. But even that victory couldn't immediately overcome some long-standing poverty consciousness. It took a few months to convince myself to buy it. But whenever my Angel-Girl sits coloring at the desk with me, the sadness doesn't have a chance.

"Daddy, the Fairy-People are flying around my room again!"

"Cool!" I call across the hall. Because of the hardwood floors throughout the house, our voices carry easily.

"They are flying around my bed in a circle. There are seven of them! What do I do?"

"Well, first say hello to them," I advise.

"I did that already, Daddy, like you taught me!"

"Did they say hello back?"

"Yup! Together, they all said, 'We greet you, Angel-Girl!'"

Author Profile

Gregory Drambour, Master Shamanic Healer, Spiritual Teacher, Author, Owner of Sedona Sacred Journeys

"If you honor them, they will honor you."

A Warrior Spirit lives within each of us! As a stage 4 cancer survivor and with thirty-six years' sobriety, Gregory embraced those powerful words and has been passing them onto thousands of clients in a healing career that has already spanned thirty years. At twenty-eight, Gregory was deeply honored to be taken under the wing of two Northern Plains Holy Men, who passed down to him eleven generations of shamanic knowledge and the warrior code. With that knowledge, Gregory began his life's work of healing and guiding clients on their Sacred Journeys and back to their innate wisdom. He is the author of *The Shaman & His Daughter* and *The Woodstock Bridge*, both considered must-reads for those wanting to go deeper into the world of old-school shamanism and practical spirituality.

For four years in his early forties, Gregory was challenged with stage 4 throat cancer. His success utilizing both alternative and conventional therapies to heal himself has drawn cancer patients and survivors from all over the world to his powerful cellular memory work. Gregory is a passionate advocate and supporter of the National Association to Protect Children and Legislative Drafting Institute for Child Protection, the only two lobbying organizations that exists for children in the United States. He has sat across from an array of clients and seen how their painful childhoods have shaped their adult lives, so he strongly believes that parenting is the key to emotional and spiritual health.

In his teaching and writing, Gregory encourages us to remember that behavior is the truth – this is the code of the warrior. It's not what you do but *how* you do it.

Also by Gregory Drambour:
The Woodstock Bridge

"A Marvelous Adventure! I Recommend It Highly!"
Richard Carlson, author of Don't Sweat The Small Stuff,
NY Times Best-Seller

A lost soul. A man desperate for meaning. Can he discover his inner Warrior and unleash the power to change?

Two decades after the heady 60s, John struggles to make sense of his life. With fading optimism, he's unsure if he can ever make a difference in the world. But crossing paths with a Sioux warrior gives him another chance for mentorship and wisdom. As John learns to confront his fears, can he find the passion that makes life worth living?

In The Woodstock Bridge: A Journey To Discover Your Spirit, he shares his hard-earned Native American wisdom to help guide you toward hope. Through simple yet powerful truths, you'll discover how to lead your spirit toward fulfillment. The Woodstock Bridge is an insightful and educational tale of spiritual empowerment. If you like intuitive teaching, inspiring stories, and expert guidance, then you'll love Gregory Drambour's catalyst for change. Buy The Woodstock Bridge to reconnect with your inner warrior!

Paperback: $14.95 • ISBN: 0-9719825-1-1
Ebook: $2.95
Available on Amazon, iBook, Barnes & Noble

Amazon link: https://tinyurl.com/woodstockbridge

Prints and other media of the photograph "Amber" are available through Wolf Mountain Images by the photographer Shari Jardina.

Website: https://www.wolfmountainimages.com/
"Amber" Order Page:
https://shari-jardina.pixels.com/featured/amber-shari-jardina.html
Shari Jardina's Links:
www.facebook.com/WolfMountainImages/
www.instagram.com/wolfmtnimages/
email: shari@wolfmountainimages.com

Author Profile

Gregory Drambour, Master Shamanic Healer, Spiritual Teacher, Author, Owner of Sedona Sacred Journeys

"If you honor them, they will honor you."

A Warrior Spirit lives within each of us! As a stage 4 cancer survivor and with thirty-six years' sobriety, Gregory embraced those powerful words and has been passing them onto thousands of clients in a healing career that has already spanned thirty years. At twenty-eight, Gregory was deeply honored to be taken under the wing of two Northern Plains Holy Men, who passed down to him eleven generations of shamanic knowledge and the warrior code. With that knowledge, Gregory began his life's work of healing and guiding clients on their Sacred Journeys and back to their innate wisdom. His books, *The Woodstock Bridge* and *The Shaman & His Daughter* are considered must reads for those wanting to go deeper into the world of old-school shamanism and practical spirituality.

For four years in his early forties, Gregory was challenged with stage 4 throat cancer. His success utilizing both alternative and conventional therapies to heal himself has drawn cancer patients and survivors from all over the world to his powerful cellular memory work. Gregory is a passionate advocate and supporter of the National Association to Protect Children and Legislative Drafting Institute for Child Protection, the only two lobbying organizations that exists for children in the United States. He has sat across from an array of clients and seen how their painful childhoods have shaped their adult lives, so he strongly believes that parenting is the key to emotional and spiritual health.

In his teaching and writing, Gregory encourages us to remember that behavior is the truth – this is the code of the warrior. It's not what you do but *how* you do it.

www.gregorydrambour.com
www.sedonasacredjourneys.com
FB: www.facebook.com/sedonasacredjourneys
IG: www.instagram.com/gregorydrambour
TW: www.twitter.com/GregDrambour

My Playlist While Writing The Book
This was the music I lived inside while writing
The Lead Guitarist & The Sisterhood of the Wolf

Iron Butterfly: In-A-Gadda-Da-Vida (this one especially)
Robert Johnson: Cross Road Blues, Kind Hearted Woman Blues, Sweet Home Chicago, Ramblin On My Mind, Come On In My Kitchen, Preachin' Blues, Hellhound On My Trail.
Son House: Grinnin' in Your Face
Chicago: Beginnings (long version), Just You 'N' Me
Kelly Joe Phelps: Goodnight Irene, Where Do I Go Now, Someone To Save Me, Fare Thee Well, Leavin' Blues, Black Crows, I've Been Converted
Argent: Hold Your Head Up
Blind Faith: Can't Find My Way Home
Janis Joplin: One Night Stand
Joe Crocker: Feelin' Alright
Elvis Presley: A Little Less Conversation
Vanilla Fudge: You Keep Me Hangin' On
Bon Dylan: Song To Woody
Dr. John: Right Place Wrong Time
Sly & The Family Stone: If You Want Me To Stay
Led Zeppelin: Dazed And Confused, No Quarter, Ten Years Gone, Rain Song (a lot!), Stairway To Heaven, Kashmir, Whole Lotta Love, In The Light. Ramble On, That's The Way
Marshall Tucker Band: Take the Highway, Can't You See
Styx: Fooling Yourself, Don't Let It End
Jimi Hendrix: Are You Experienced, Purple Haze, Along The

Watchtower, Hear My Train Comin', Fire, The Wind Cries
Mary, Foxy Lady, Hey Joe
Elton John: Bennie And The Jets
John Cafferty & The Beaver Brown Band: Maryia
The Allman Brothers Band: Melissa
The Rolling Stones: Can't You Hear Me Knocking
Rare Earth: I Just Want To Celebrate
The Doors: Peace Frog
Jefferson Airplane: White Rabbit
Bad Company: Bad Company
Mountain: Mississippi Queen
Steppenwolf: Magic Carpet Ride, Born To Be Wild, The Pusher
Lakota Thunder: Looking for My Friend (A Lot!)
Cat Stevens: Bitterblue, Peace Train, Miles From Nowhere
Free: All Right Now

Made in the USA
Monee, IL
03 May 2020